LOST GREAT FALLS

KEN ROBISON

THE History PRESS

Published by The History Press
An imprint of Arcadia Publishing
Charleston, SC
www.historypress.com

Front cover: *Great Falls Remembered*, painted by Brian Morger, depicts the 506-foot Anaconda Copper Company Smokestack, an iconic landmark, built in 1911 and demolished in 1976 despite community efforts to "Save Our Stack." *Courtesy of Tom and Mary Jane Heisler Family.*

First published 2025

Manufactured in the United States

ISBN 9781467157803

Library of Congress Control Number: 2025933740

For Ellen and Ken Sievert, who have shared their knowledge and passion for historic preservation with me and with our Great Falls/Cascade County community for many years.

And here's to Ira "Ike" M. Kaufman Jr., who knew downtown Great Falls to perfection. Rest in peace.

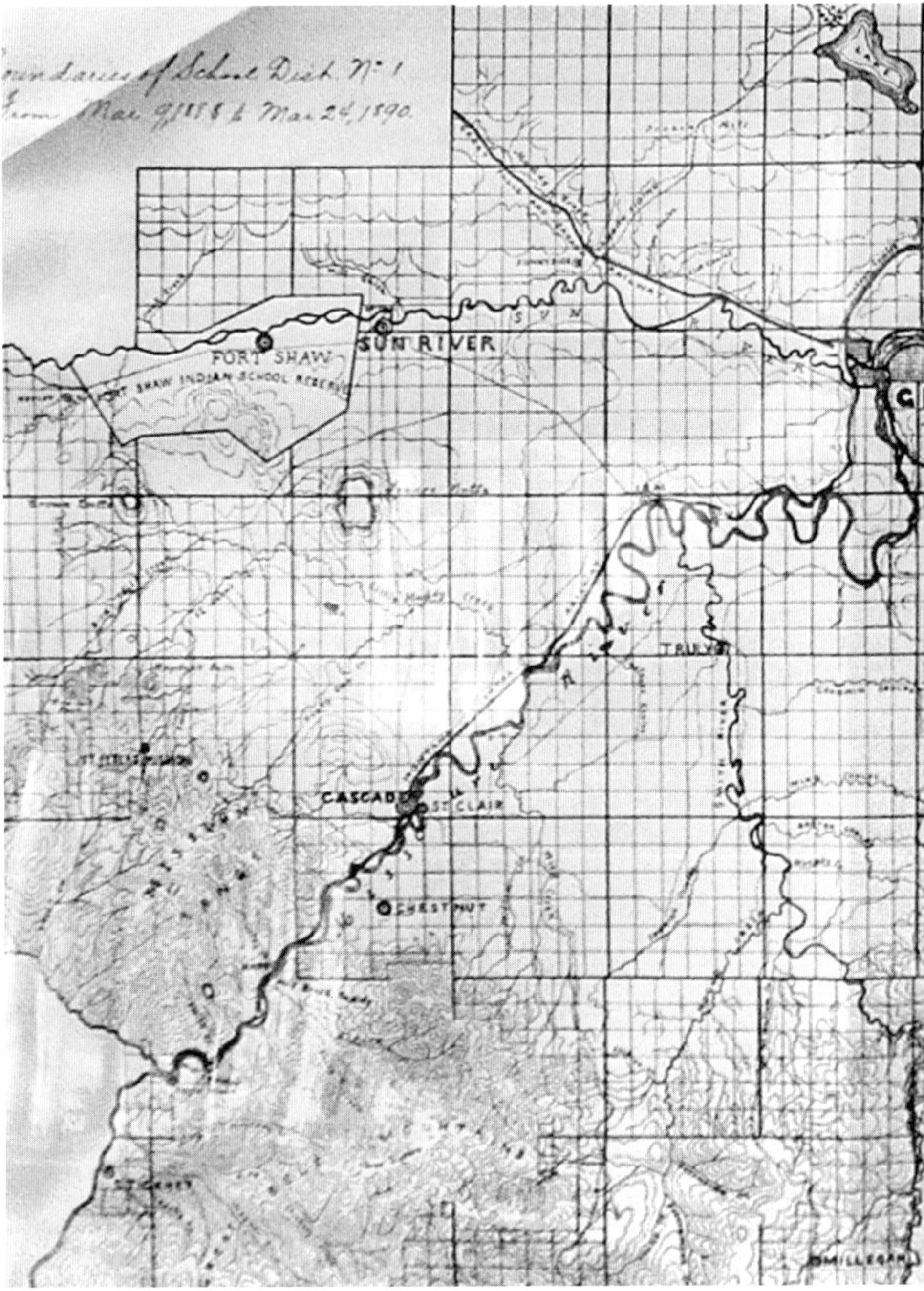

Map of Cascade County in 1896 by O.C. Mortson. *Author collection.*

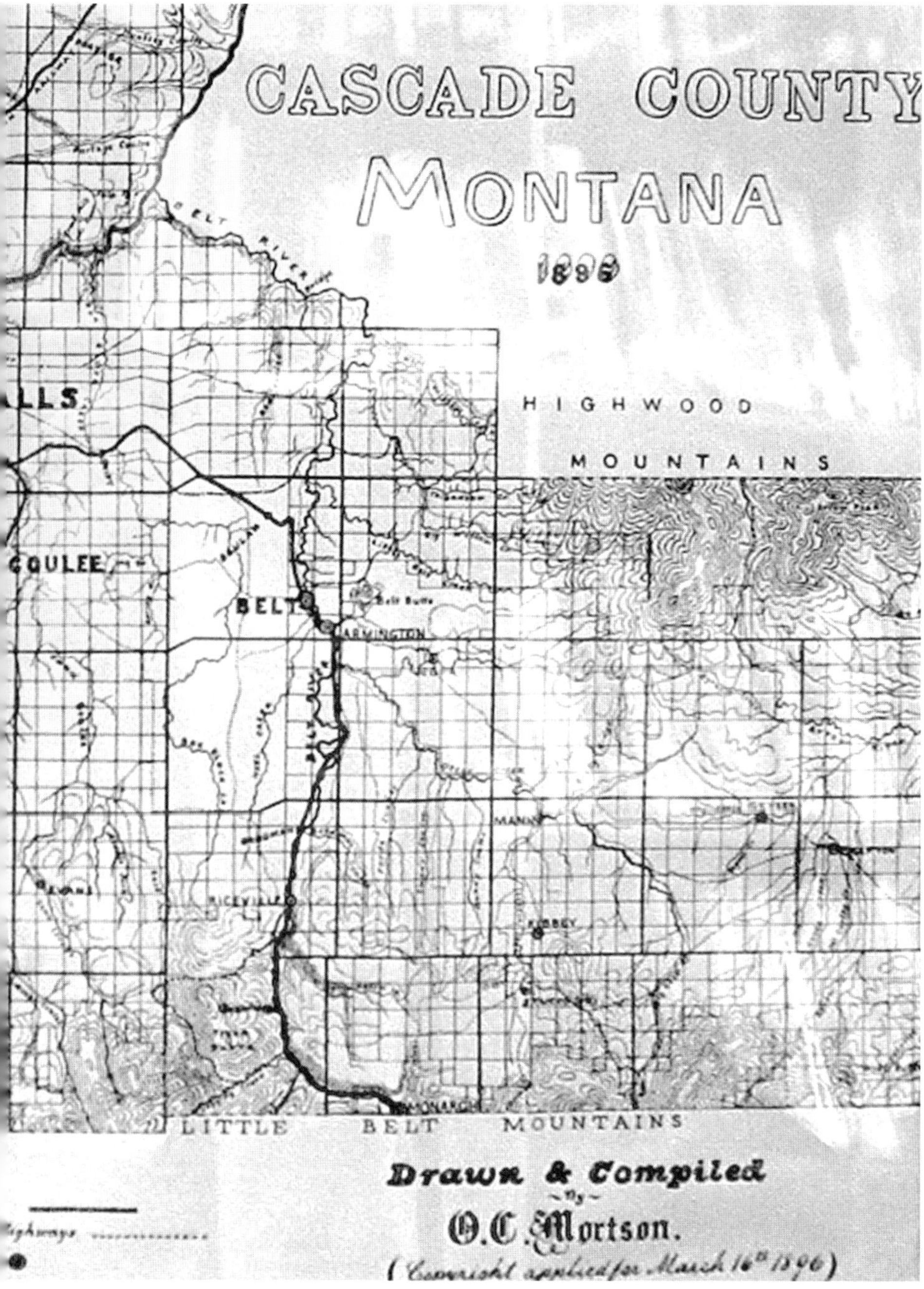

CASCADE COUNTY
MONTANA
HIGHWOOD
MOUNTAINS
BELT RIVER
LLS
COULEE
BELT
ARMINGTON
MANN
RICEVILLE
MONARCH
LITTLE BELT MOUNTAINS
Drawn & Compiled
by
O. C. Mortson.
(Copyright applied for March 16th 1896)

CONTENTS

INTRODUCTION

From its beginning, Great Falls was more than a city of "wind, water, and future," as Montana's pioneer towns derisively called it. With Paris Gibson's arrival on the upper Missouri River at Fort Benton, Montana Territory, in 1879, the birth of a city at the five falls of the Missouri became inevitable. Gibson had observed the growth of Minneapolis from village to city in just two decades. After viewing the incomparable falls of the Missouri and discussing the potential with old-timers, Paris Gibson determined to found a "Minneapolis at the Falls."

Deep in the heart of Blackfoot country, the bend in the Missouri River had long served as the transportation corridor for thousands of buffalo and Indigenous people from many tribes crossing a natural ford in the river above the falls connecting the Sun River Valley and the broad Judith Basin. Fueled by nearby silver and coal resources and powered by hydroelectricity from dams on the falls, Great Falls became a rapidly growing planned city within a decade. In little more than half a century, the Electric City became Montana's largest city, undergoing dramatic growth first from its copper refining industry that literally "wired the world" and then from the homestead boom that formed the Golden Triangle for agriculture with its massive waves of grain. Topping off the growth two decades later came the sudden extensive military presence brought on by World War II and the Cold War.

As suddenly as it grew, Great Falls declined dramatically during the late 1970s and '80s with the loss of heavy industry and railroad repair yards.

An 1891 perspective map of Great Falls revealing its dramatic growth in just seven years.
Author collection.

MISSOURI RIVER
SUN RIVER

Consequently, few cities have ever fostered a greater nostalgia for their past: a yearning for the way things once were in Great Falls during those fondly recalled decades of dramatic growth.

Nostalgia tends to magnify the memory of the good of the past as Great Falls remembers those moments when it was most alive, treasuring what was then, lamenting the perceived end of those "good times."

Lost Great Falls aims to capture the romantic notion of what has been lost to time and failed preservation, presenting an illustrative collection of important buildings no longer standing, marquees gone dark, railways abandoned and communities vanished. This book chronicles the bygone physical, cultural and social aspects of life in Great Falls, from the faded memories of that ancient strategic ford across the Missouri and of Johnstown, the first rival of the new Great Falls townsite, to the 1982 morale-crushing demolition of the Big Stack, that iconic landmark and symbol of the great industrial past.

Symbolic of the many preservation failures over the years is the failed attempt to preserve and restore the town's one-room first schoolhouse. Urban renewal destroyed two blocks of the most historic buildings in downtown Great Falls, including the Minot Block, home of the first Cascade County and city offices, the Electric City Club with its beloved African American steward, the popular but long-forgotten Alcazar Theater, Hussman's Cigar Store and the city's two most famous saloons, the Silver Dollar and the Mint, renowned as "watering holes" for "Cowboy Artist" Charlie Russell and his friends and for their presentation of his priceless art.

Oldtimers lament the loss of the city's first public library, the Valeria, named for Paris Gibson's wife, and the first brewery opened by the Volk Brothers with its amazing legacy as the training camp for heavyweight boxing champion Jack Dempsey and the nightclub inn, the Dempsey Inn, named for the champ.

Few remember two railway operations that fostered the dramatic growth of the city. The first was the Great Falls & Canada Railway, which played a role in the tragic 1896 deportation of the Cree from Montana. That narrow-gauge "Turkey Trail" railroad not only symbolized the closely shared heritage between Great Falls and the Canadian "prairie provinces" but also accelerated the settlement of the rich agricultural Golden Triangle in northern Montana. The second was the Great Falls Street Railway, with its streetcars moving shoppers and workers around the city before the era of buses and automobiles.

The opening of the Grand Opera House in 1892, when the city was less than a decade old, symbolized the dramatic growth of the 1890s and featured the superstars of the day, like Mark Twain, who endured the worst performance night of his long career there after being enchanted by the little city's beauty and natural features like the Giant Springs. The fading grandeur of the Grand Opera could not save it from the overactive demolition "wrecking ball."

As designed in the Great Falls 1883 survey map, through the years, parkland was featured throughout the city. The earliest entertainment center was at Black Eagle Park, where events and sports abounded. From the first basketball games by the Fort Shaw Indian School girls' team to the first aerial flight in the city and Fort Assinniboine cavalry demonstrations, Black Eagle Park, operated by the Street Railway, presented entertainment of all kinds.

In Gibson Park, the city's finest, a Zoological Gardens opened to the delight of children and enjoyment of all. Wolves, coyotes, elk, deer and antelope roamed their enclosures, while on Gibson Lake, a wide variety of waterfowl, including swans, paddled and flew around.

Few stories have been lost as quietly as that of Tenth Alley South, a city- and railroad-sponsored block of brick "mansions" housing the city's "ladies of the night" in fine style.

Within a few decades, lavish entertainment theaters opened, including the last in the famed series of West Coast vaudeville theaters of Alexander Pantages and the plush pleasure palace the Liberty Theatre, both lost to the world of television and home entertainment. Luther's Dance Hall hosted a wide range of events, from grand balls to indoors homecourt for Fort Shaw girls' basketball, before its reuse as the longtime Eagles Lodge. Meanwhile, briefly lighting the cultural scene was one of Montana's finest antiquarian bookstores, Fireside Books.

The seedy lower Southside with its multiethnic and multicultural residents became a "jungle" of bars and joints of all kinds, including, remarkably, the finest African American jazz club between Chicago and Seattle, the Ozark Club, where leading Black performers from Lionel Hampton to Redd Foxx to "Miss Wiggles" spent the nighttime hours entertaining Black and White servicemen, couples and businessmen in an environment where "everyone is welcome" at a time when not everyone was welcome at other restaurants and nightclubs.

After the closure of Anaconda Copper Company's refineries, the iconic 506-foot landmark Big Stack, the symbol of the city, was demolished despite a robust attempt to "Save Our Stack." With this, the end of Great Falls' heavy industry and its revered symbol, the city dove into decades of decline from which it is just now recovering.

My special thanks to Megan Sanford, curator at The History Museum, for key images and to Samantha Long, Great Falls/Cascade County Historic Preservation Commission historic preservation officer, for images and architectural drawings.

Much more has been lost from the city's scene over the years, such as the glorious Christmastime at the Paris Department Store, the powerful Rainbow Power House, the vibrant DeMolay Memorial, the oldest apartment, Linden Terrace, the important YMCA and Saint Thomas Orphanage, home to the homeless. More today are endangered, like Smelter Hill's last surviving structure, the Boston and Montana Barn, the anchor Rocky Mountain Fire Insurance Building on one side of downtown Great Falls and the integrity of the Great Falls Lewis and Clark Portage National Historic Landmark.

As you read these stories, feeling the sentimental emotions of pleasure with a touch of sadness when you think about the lost places and events of Great Falls past, remember and celebrate the preservation successes, such as the Avon Block with its Celtic Cowboy and Avon Hotel; the Vinegar Jones Cabin, Great Falls' "first home"; and the many buildings being restored and reused in downtown Great Falls today—and, perhaps, encourage a community rededication to preserve and protect our most cherished places in the future.

Chapter 1

GREAT FALLS FORD

Deep in the heart of Blackfoot country where the city of Great Falls stands today, for thousands of years, immense herds of buffalo crossed the Missouri River on their way from the high plains along the eastern front of the Rockies to their winter grazing grounds in the Judith Basin and Musselshell Valley. On their seasonal rounds, the Blackfoot and other Indigenous peoples who lived on the plains east of the Rockies followed the buffalo. Additionally, the Confederated Salish and Kootenai and Pend d'Oreille and other tribes from the valleys west of the Rockies, where there were no bison, crossed the mountains on hunting expeditions.

The natural river ford featured an excellent low-water crossing with a sloped bedrock bottom that was easy to enter and exit. The ford was located between today's Great Northern Railway Bridge and the First Avenue North Highway Bridge and crossed the river directly above the first rapids above Black Eagle Falls. This ford was the only shallow crossing for nearly forty miles in either direction and was marked by deep-worn trails. The Apsáalooke Crow tribe frequently came northwest to hunt the buffalo, and it was inevitable that the region near the ford should be the scene of bloody encounters between the hostile tribes that met and clashed there.

Artist Les Peters's painting of a bison herd crossing the ford on the Missouri River at Great Falls on its way to the Sun River Valley. *Author collection.*

FIRST PEOPLES BUFFALO JUMP STATE PARK AND NATIONAL HISTORIC LANDMARK

According to early rancher Robert Ford, Blackfoot elders told him that the Sun River Valley was the best game country west of the Mississippi and, therefore, the scene of continual wars for its possession. About ten miles beyond the ford, south of the Sun River, is the immense natural *piskun* known as the First Peoples Buffalo Jump State Park and National Historic Landmark, likely the largest buffalo cliff jump in the world; human activity there dates to at least 500 AD. This piskun, a Blackfeet word meaning "deep blood kettle," had five features: the area where bison grazed; the "drive lane," with two rock lines about ten yards apart and up to one mile in length; the cliff some thirty to fifty feet above a rocky slope where the Natives killed the bison that survived the fall; and the camp where the hunters lived while harvesting the bison. Archaeological evidence reveals that some thirteen Indigenous nations used this piskun over the centuries.[1]

CATTLE CROSSING THE FORD

In 1878, Wyllys Hedges filed on a tract of land that later became part of west Great Falls. He later moved to the Musselshell Valley to continue ranching in 1881 and became speaker of the Montana House of Representatives. His great-nephew Geoffrey L. Brazier of Helena found Hedges's reminiscences

The ford across the Missouri River today, looking east. *Author photo.*

among family papers, including this account of crossing the Great Falls ford with a large cattle herd.

Cattle Forded River Near Broadwater Bay

Hay was not very plentiful, but we cut what we could get in the swales and bottoms (on the homestead on what is now Great Falls' Westside).

While thus engaged early in August 1880, we had a call from a cattleman named Gallagher who was moving a herd of mixed cattle numbering some 2,000 head. He inquired about the ford across the Missouri River. We told him it was an excellent crossing, water low with bedrock bottom easy to enter and low easy place opposite to come out on.

He asked if we could help him to cross his herd. There were four men in our outfit. We suggested that he hold his herd out away from water all night. And that we would work a while next morning but would stop at 9:30 or 10 o'clock, saddle up and help him over.

He was to keep his herd well together till he came near the ford, then rope two or three calves and put them in the cook wagon, drive right into the water and cross. It was presumed the mothers of the calves would follow very closely and thus take the lead in crossing, which they did of course.

There was little trouble in getting the herd started and clear over to opposite side. But when you have 2,000 head of mixed cattle, calves, yearlings, and everything going into a rather rapid current of that width it is easy to see that there will be a great mix-up. The young stock gets carried downstream and come out on either side. They get separated from mothers and companions and considerably excited. All but the steers do much bawling, and they add to the general hubbub and racket.

It was hard on horses which frequently got out of their depth and had to swim more or less.

The job took till past noon to get the last head over, and men and horses were very glad of a rest with the noon meal prepared by the camp cook of the herd. You can take our word that it tasted good, even if seasoned with considerable dust and dirt. Gallagher wanted to pay us for our assistance. But that was not the custom in those days. The range men always helped one another under such circumstances, always expected to do so.[2]

JEEP ACROSS THE MISSOURI

A wagon bridge built in 1888 ended the use and danger of the nearby Great Falls ford. Almost one hundred years later, and long after the ford had last seen heavy traffic by bison and cattle, Pete Rice of Rice Motors determined to find out if he could ford the river in his Jeep, and according to the *Great Falls Tribune*,

> *Sure enough, he did. Starting early Thursday so no one would see a possible failure, he drove* [his Jeep] *into the Missouri River from the east at a point about 100 yards north of the…railroad bridge. After one false start he succeeded in crossing the river.*[3]

Chapter 2

JOHNSTOWN

Well, it seemed a good idea at the time. In the summer of 1883, while Herbert P. Rolfe and his crew were on the ground surveying the townsite of Great Falls, the "future great," a hopeful settlement, Johnstown, was already rising on the opposite (west) bank of the Missouri River. Johnstown, named for Sun River merchant John Largent, was already underway just west of the ancient ford of the Missouri and north of the Sun River at a site where the Great Northern roundhouse and shops would be located in later years.[1]

In 1883, Johnstown had business all to itself and consisted of a stage stop, a general store and a barn. The site seemed ideal since it was on the direct road between Sun River and the Judith Basin settlements. Access to the "future great" on the other side of the Missouri required either a ferry ride, a very wet crossing of the ford or a long wait for a future bridge across the river.[5]

John Largent and his brother Edward "Bert" Largent recorded a plat in what was then Choteau County on April 17, 1884, as proprietors of the townsite of Johnstown. Witnesses were Sun River rancher Robert S. Ford and Lansing S. Wells. John M. Marsh had surveyed the townsite earlier, and it consisted of fifteen blocks bordered by Sun River Street, running east to west. Bert Largent operated the small settlement.[6]

A Mr. Anthony remembered hauling three loads of coal to Bert Largent's little store at Johnstown in 1883 and taking his pay in groceries. In a letter forty-six years later, Allen Pierse wrote,

> *Mrs. Pierse and myself stopped across the river opposite the present site of Great Falls at a place called Johnstown. The town, as we remember, consisted of one house, and the proprietor carried a small stock of merchandise and accommodated anyone who might want to spend the night there. The following morning, we crossed the Missouri river on a ferry to where Great Falls is now located. Not a building was here at that time. We met Paris Gibson who had driven up from Fort Benton in his buggy....He told us the day was not far distant when there would be a city built where we were then standing. It seemed like a dream.*[7]

During the first year of the Great Falls townsite in 1884, before it had a single store or a newspaper, the *Sun River Sun* advertised the Johnstown store of "E.B. Largent and Co. Dealers in General Merchandise, Groceries, Dry Goods, Boots & Shoes, Clothing and Hardware." A restaurant and post office were added to its facilities, and regular stage service began between Johnstown and Sun River town. Sam Getts drove the "jerky" coming through every other day.[8]

In the spring of 1884, under Paris Gibson's guidance, the construction of the new townsite of Great Falls began. Travelers arrived at Johnstown and continued to the "future great" via the ford in low water and or the ferry in high water. Both were located just north of the future Great Northern (now Burlington Northern) bridge, connecting near Fourth Avenue Southwest on the Westside, as Johnstown later became known. At the time, Paris Gibson and other early residents of Great Falls lived in tents or temporary shacks. A small log cabin built by Josiah Peeper, later known as the Vinegar Jones Cabin, became the first permanent structure in Great Falls. [9]

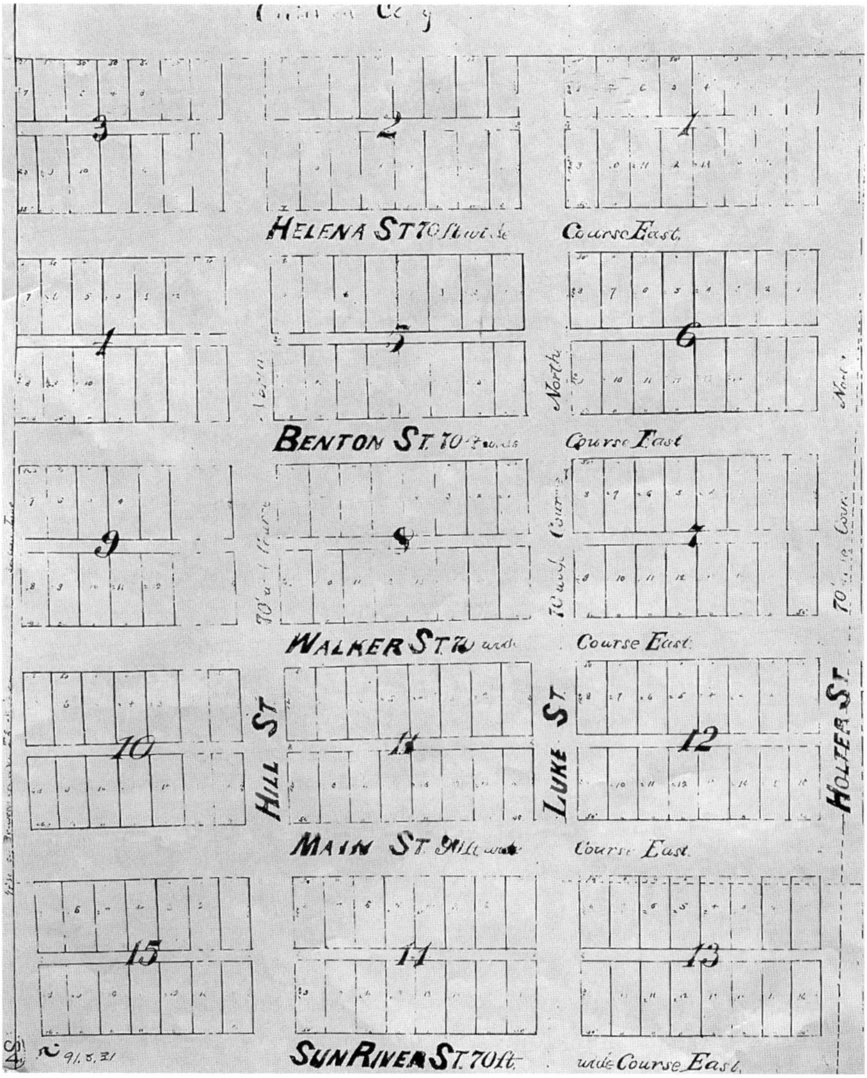

Opposite: In 1884, the new Great Falls townsite and its rival, Johnstown, located to the west just across the Missouri River, were connected only by this ferry, except when low water permitted fording the stream. *From the* Fairfield Times, *January 18, 1929.*

Above: Plat of the townsite of Johnstown, Choteau County. *The History Museum (hereafter THM).*

A sketch by "Rube" Hildebrand of the Largent store in Johnstown and the stage arriving from Fort Benton. *From the* Great Falls Tribune *(hereafter* Tribune*), March 7, 1915.*

As Great Falls slowly began to grow, Johnstown—with its general store and restaurant; its post office, where Bert Largent served as postmaster; and regular stagecoach service to and from Sun River and on to Helena, the territorial capital—briefly prospered. Grant McKain opened a saloon in Johnstown, several lots were sold and many trees were planted. Johnson Goon used the ferry to bring mail from the Johnstown Post Office to Great Falls for delivery to homes as far away as Sand Coulee.[10]

Yet the fall of Johnstown was inevitable, and over the next several years, Great Falls, backed by railroad man James J. Hill, big money interests in Minneapolis and the driving will of Paris Gibson, grew, while Johnstown did not. The *Sun River Sun* moved to Great Falls and became the *Tribune*, and the *Tribune* editorialized:

> *Johnstown is no more. The last of the Johnstownites moved to Great Falls Thursday of this week* [October 7]. *Thus is the "future great" depleting all the surrounding towns.*[11]

In 1891, Johnstown Townsite was transferred to the Great Falls Townsite Company. The name Johnstown persisted, remaining on the railway station until 1905, when the sign came down and the depot became a yard office. Over time, the area came to be known as West Great Falls. The onetime good idea and promising town of Johnstown was no more.[12]

Chapter 3

FIRST SCHOOLHOUSE

In early June 1885, supported by modest public subscription, master carpenter and contractor Whitman Gibson "Vinegar" Jones prepared the excavation and S.S. Whittier began building a twenty-by-forty-foot one-story wood-frame school. Mary Johnstone Powers described the events leading up to this first schoolhouse in Great Falls:

> *In the fall of 1884, I was elected County Superintendent of Schools in Choteau County....Shortly after taking office, a petition came to me from the little village of Great Falls, praying that I recommend the setting off of the Great Falls District from the County District of Sand Coulee, and, if granted, the names of those desired as clerk and trustees were given. The same day I read the petition, a Mr. Field and Professor* [O.C.] *Mortson had come to Benton to protest against the new district, as they claimed the village of Great Falls could not support a school, neither could they build a schoolhouse, and that the Sand Coulee district, being a rich district of stockmen, could build the schoolhouse and run the school to a better advantage of all.*
>
> *After consulting with a few people, I decided to recommend the formation of the Great Falls District....My recommendation was approved by the County Commissioners of Choteau County, so I proceeded to name the following trustees: Mr. Paris Gibson, H.P. Rolfe, J.T. Lee, and Mr.* [Silas A.] *Beachley, clerk....*

Above: Great Falls' First School, a one-room schoolhouse, completed by contractor S.S. Whittier in October 1885. *Author collection.*

Opposite: Whitman Gibson (W.G.) Jones, known as "Vinegar" Jones, cousin of Great Falls founder Paris Gibson and an early master carpenter and contractor. *Author collection.*

> *After the formation of the Great Falls District, the first Board of Trustees meeting of District No. 9, Choteau County, was held on September 8, 1885. Paris Gibson was elected Chairman.…J.M. Largent was…offered whatever amount of money is appertained to this District for the next 9 months, not to exceed $900, to teach 9 months in this District.*[13]

After a very slow beginning in 1884, the tiny townsite of Great Falls began to transform the prairie into a town during 1885. The greatest achievement that second year was the erection, by public contribution, of a tiny one-room schoolhouse. The 1923 Great Falls High School *Round-Up* paid tribute to that first school:

> *The citizens of Great Falls called a mass meeting…for the purpose of determining how, without funds to any large amount, a building could be erected for the instruction of the ever-growing youth of this fair Electric City. It was unanimously agreed that there must be a schoolhouse of some kind the following fall.…The site for the building…on Third Avenue South and Fifth Street, was donated by the townsite company, and the materials and work were apportioned among the citizens.*[14]
>
> *Led by Whittier, through the summer construction of the school continued, halting intermittently for lack of building material.*[15]

TRUSTEES ORGANIZE

On September 1, the school trustees Rolfe, James T. Lee and Paris Gibson of District No. 9 held their first meeting, electing Gibson chairman. The trustees voted to offer Reverend James M. Largent the position of teacher and to have the school term commence "as soon as the schoolhouse is finished." A nine-month school term was agreed on, and the Townsite Company prepared to deed the lot to the district. In addition to the small resident population, several families prepared to move into town for the winter to send their children to school.[16]

SCHOOL OPENS

The plasterers completed their work, and the little schoolhouse was ready for the Great Falls public school to open on Monday, October 12, "with a good attendance," to be augmented shortly by pupils coming in from Sand Coulee and other sections.[17]

The First School report for the month ending November 13 showed nineteen students on the roll: nine girls and ten boys. Teacher Largent reported:

As this is the first school in the place not much was anticipated in the way of a "big" school, but the above report is not so bad to begin with. Many hindrances to the success of a first-class school have been overcome and we got to work with great hopes for the future. Many visitors are always welcome.[18]

FIRST CHRISTMAS CELEBRATION

From the beginning, the little schoolhouse hosted community gatherings as well; the Reverend Largent had begun church services and Sunday school by the end of October. For two years, the Presbyterian church also held services there, until a church was built. Additionally, school elections, political conventions and precinct elections were held in the little schoolhouse.[19]

As December 1885 approached, planning began for the first Christmas celebration in Great Falls. Kate Beachley remembered the previous year, the first year of the townsite. In her words,

> *I well remember our first Christmas here. We did not have any celebration whatever. I remember that Mrs.* [Rozina See] *Wamer was here, and Howard Criss, H.* [Herbert] *O. Chowen, Bert Huy, Phil. Gibson, and a few others, but the town was very small, and Christmas passed unobserved. I spent the day in studying the Bible.*
>
> *The next year* [1885], *we had the first celebration in Great Falls, with a Christmas tree in the old frame schoolhouse, Third avenue south and Fifth street. People came from miles around for that Christmas tree, and there were presents for everybody. We were living then at the northeast corner of Central avenue and Fourth street. In the front of the building, we had the postoffice and a stock of stationery and confectionery, and we lived in a little room to the rear of the store.*
>
> *When it was decided to have a Christmas celebration, we sent to Helena for things to place on the tree, and no one was forgotten. Word was sent out all over the surrounding country, wherever there were settlers, and people came from as far away as Belt.*
>
> *The weather was very pleasant. I remember that when Mr. and Mrs.* [Will] *Junkins came in, they came to our house—it was a sort of general stopping place. Frank Junkins was a baby then, and I remember that we had little room, and when his mother carried him into the house, she sat him*

on the stove. The day was so warm that we did not need any fire. I know I had been baking early in the day and it was so hot that I kept the windows open until the fire had gone out.

I do not remember all who were present at that first Christmas tree, but I recall many. All the town people were there, and among those who came in from the country were the Junkinses, the Hamiltons, the Lees, the Goons, the Fields, the Ladds, the Walkers, the Gehrings, the Chichesters, Ira Hickory, and S.A. Beachly.

Professor [O.C.] *Mortson was Santa Claus that year, and the house was packed when he began to distribute the presents. The tree was laden with candy, nuts, popcorn, and articles of all descriptions. There was a barrel of apples in the room, and everybody was invited to have one.*

Music was furnished by Mr. and Mrs. Junkins, who had an organ, and that music was one of the delightful features of the entertainment.

I can't remember much about the presents. I do remember well, though, one that Bert Huy and I gave to W. [Worden] *P. Wren, and I think Mr. Wren was mad about it. Several days before Christmas, Mr. Huy came to me and asked me to make a doll, to be placed on the Christmas tree for Mr. Wren. I told him I did not have anything with which to make a doll, but he insisted, and finally I fashioned one from a pillow slip, and it was placed on the tree. Mr. Wren thought Tom Carter was going to get it and was greatly amused, but when the doll was tossed to him, I think he was disgusted.*

There were a good many settlers up the Sun River Valley then, but I cannot recall that any from that direction were present at that Christmas tree. They probably went to Sun River. You see, there was no bridge across the river then. We even had to go across on the ferry to Johnstown to get our mail. Mr. Goon used to go across and get the mail, bring it over and then ride to the homes between here and Sand Coulee, making the distribution.[20]

The little schoolhouse was tastefully decorated, and the tree, with its weight of presents, glistened and sparkled in the light of numerous wax candles. The large crowd assembled at the schoolhouse on Christmas night greatly enjoyed the exercises performed by the Sunday school scholars.[21]

MORE STUDENTS

By the spring of 1886, student enrollment had edged up to twenty-four, and more than fifty students had begun to crowd the school by Christmas that year. Reverend Largent continued as teacher until May 1887, when he was replaced by Sarah A. McBrine. By October 1887, enrollment had exceeded the limits of the school. A second teacher, Jessie Rich, experienced teaching in Helena schools, was hired, and a second school was opened. Miss Rich taught the lower grades at the schoolhouse, while Miss McBrine led the higher grades in the Lapeyre building on Central Avenue.[22]

Cascade County separated from Choteau County in the autumn of 1887. School District No. 1 was organized on March 9, 1888. A new board of trustees, composed of members H.P. Rolfe, Charles Wagner, Joseph Jelica and clerk Eli Ringwald, met one week later. The first action of the new board was to post notice of a bond election for construction of a $20,000 schoolhouse to be held in April. The bond passed, and by October, a two-story brick and stone school was under construction at the corner of Eighth Street and Third Avenue North; it was later named Whittier School.[23]

During 1888, teacher Rich continued with the lower grades at the old school and teacher McBrine with the higher grades at the Lapeyre building. In September, Fannie Ewing arrived from Deer Lodge to replace Miss McBrine, moving her higher-grade students to the Beachley building on Central Avenue.[24]

The school building served many years as a commercial grocery store. *Author collection.*

With Whittier School still under construction, in the spring of 1889, Miss Rich had fifty students in the old school, while Miss Ewing had the same number at the Beachley School. In August, yet a third school opened as Mrs. Holbrook was hired to teach the winter term on the Westside of the Missouri River. J.G. Thompson was hired as principal for the district schools, and in the fall, there were seventy-three scholars in the new Whittier School, while Miss Rich remained at the old one-room school with forty-three students. The old school closed operations in 1891 with all students consolidated at Whittier School. During the 1890s, Great Falls boomed, and the number of schoolchildren increased dramatically.[25]

MANY LIVES

The First School building was reused in many ways over the years, serving first as a grocery store and later as a private residence. For more than a decade, the school remained active, hosting school board meetings and elections and political gatherings. In 1893, a Mrs. Conner operated a sewing school in the building. In 1901, the *Leader* reported on the deteriorating state of the building during a spring school election:

> *The old school house, while still picturesque as a landmark, has lost any good qualities which it might have had as a place of comfort, and while the female judge and clerk shivered from the winds which blew gently through the open windows, the male portion of the official family went out and stole a few lumps of coal, smashed it with a club and having no wash basin was compelled to mop over the books with his toil-stained hands—and the lady judges shivered to the end of the chapter.*[26]

Minor repairs kept the First School in use. The first known commercial tenant, the Idlewild Creamery, moved into the front of the building in 1907; there were residential apartments in the back. Many businesses followed: the Boss Café, featuring "Japanese Chop Suey and Noodles," in 1910; Harley-Davidson Sales in 1912; from 1913 onward, several grocery stores: Smock, Dunlop, Arcade; Haefer Furs, from 1925 to 1931; several grocers in quick succession during the 1930s; and Lincoln Grocery, the last grocer to occupy the building, in the early 1940s. From then on, the First School served as a residential building.

SAVING FIRST SCHOOL

By the 1970s, Grogan-Robinson Lumber Company owned the First School, and it stood in the way of the company's planned expansion. J. Brooks Robinson offered to donate the building to the newly formed Cascade County Historical Society, then based at Paris Gibson Square—the former Central High School and later Paris Gibson Junior High. Directors of the square confirmed the historical significance of the building and offered it a temporary home, so the historical society agreed to move and renovate it rather than have the First School torn down. Preservationist Charles A. Bovey offered assistance in moving the building and raising money for restoration.[27]

In June 1978, the First School was moved to Paris Gibson Square. Bovey's associate John Ellingsen prepared specifications for the restoration of the interior, including removing existing interior partitions and the building's false ceiling, retaining the original wainscoting, replacing the blackboard above the wainscoting and installing new sheetrock on the wall above the blackboard and on the ceiling. Historical society volunteers began preservation work.[28]

LOST FIRST SCHOOL

Another year passed, and the historical society failed to find a permanent site for the First School. The Paris Gibson Square directors demanded that the First School be moved since it did not conform to the site plan for preservation of the square. Final efforts for relocation failed in March 1980, and Great Falls' First School was demolished.[29]

Chapter 4

MINOT BLOCK

In the fall of 1887, Henry D. Minot began construction of a fine three-story block for offices on the north side of Central Avenue at 201–203. Minot, a Boston-born capitalist, moved to St. Paul in the early 1880s and became president of the Eastern Railroad of Minnesota and director of the Manitoba Railroad. His investment in the future of Great Falls was short-lived; he was killed in a train wreck on the Pennsylvania Railroad near Pittsburg in November 1890. By mid-November 1887, the Minot Block, constructed by E.V. Boughton under the supervision of architect F.M. Morgan, was nearing completion. The Minot Block, commonly called Central Block, assumed great importance in the early years of Great Falls, housing the offices of the newly formed Cascade County government, including the sheriff's office, the city council chambers, the important Electric City Club and the First National Bank of Great Falls.[30]

NEW MINOT BLOCK

The *Tribune* described the new Minot Block:

> *The Central block is approaching completion. The plastering is nearly finished, and the wood work is such as can be done in either rough or fair weather. The building can be seen from a long distance and adds considerably to the general appearance of Central avenue.*

Architectural rendering of the Minot Block. *From the* Tribune, *November 11, 1959.*

In the foundation spacious vaults have been built and ample space has been allotted to the cellars, which are deep and well ventilated.

The first floor is divided into two suites of offices. It has a large door in the center whence the hall leads to space for an elevator, which will be the first of the kind introduced here. The First National Bank of Great Falls has rented the west side of this floor from front to rear. A door has been opened for the bank in addition to the main one. As originally designed the space required by the bank included a front office 20 × 22 feet, another office 16 × 14, an apartment 16 × 20 and another 10½ × 12 feet. The bank has had this arrangement modified so as to give a spacious counting-house and rooms for the directors and cashier. All these will be finished in solid, substantial style, and when furnished will equal any in the territory in facilities for business, as well as insensible, judicious adornment. The bank will have spacious vaults, with massive cement floors insuring ample protection against fire and burglars.

The other side of the first floor is nominally divided into two offices, one of which is 20 feet square and the other 20 by 36 feet, with a large vault adjoining. These offices may, however, be turned into a large storeroom as there is only a railing between them. The store would be 20 feet in front by 56 in length and would afford ample space for carrying on a large business.

THE SECOND FLOOR

Stairs of very easy ascent lead to the second floor which has been rented by Cascade county and will contain spacious offices for the public officials thereof. Good light and excellent ventilation, with fine views, are leading features in these apartments, which will provide abundant accommodation for the public business until Cascade county erects a building of her own, which will combine a city hall, court rooms and perhaps a library and public hall. The plan divides this floor into seven offices, but some changes are being made to adapt the offices to the several departments of the county business. It is deemed fortunate that this fine building will be ready for use before Cascade county acquires legal existence. The combination of all the offices on one spacious floor will promote the public convenience. People will be able to pay taxes, record deeds and consult the sheriff, county attorney or public administrator without the delay entailed when these officials transact business in different buildings.

THE THIRD FLOOR

On the Central avenue front of the third floor are three large rooms with closets large enough to please any householder. There is another large room on the west side and one with a skylight on the east. At the back is the ball room or public hall. This room is 48½ feet long by 25 feet wide, and is thus admirably adapted for social gatherings, church fairs or public meetings. The room is well proportioned and does not present that aspect of vacancy which mars the effect of ballrooms when they are not well filled.

Provision is made in several of the rooms for fireplaces as well as stoves. The ceilings are to correspond with the reaction which has set in against those high ceilings which have been so common in large cities. For ventilation and comfort the ceilings are high enough. There is a light and ventilator shaft from the first floor to the top of the building. Provision will be made

The 201 address block on Central Avenue, about 1906, with the Minot Block (*left*) on the corner lot, the Alcazar Theater in the Dunn Block on the next lot and the Silver Dollar Saloon four lots east. *Author collection.*

> *for gas or electric light and all modern improvements will be introduced in the plumber work.*
>
> *This building has a frontage of 50 feet and a depth of 60 feet. Its height from foundation to the roof is 55 feet. It is built of brick made here. The main part of the timber work has also been procured here. The contract has been carried out successfully by Mr. Boughton under the supervision of Mr. Morgan. The owner Mr. Minot of Boston is largely interested in the Burlington and Manitoba railways.*
>
> *This fine structure is the product of home enterprise and home labor. The brick and stone and lumber have all been procured here. Including the lot, the building will represent when complete an investment of $25,000 and will pay a liberal annual income thereon. It will lead, no doubt, in the construction of other blocks on the same extensive scale.*[31]

FORMING CASCADE COUNTY

Until September 12, 1887, Great Falls had been part of Choteau County.[32] The contentious formation of the new Cascade County with Great Falls as county seat has been described as follows:

> *Keen interest was aroused in 1887 in the proposed new county of Cascade to be formed from portions of Meagher, Lewis and Clark, and Choteau counties. The population of Great Falls having reached 1,200 at the beginning of the year, the town initiated a movement to make it the county seat. The bill was presented at an extraordinary session of the legislature convened by Governor Preston H. Leslie, and although it met with considerable opposition from residents from Sun River region and business bodies of Helena and Fort Benton, it passed. The county officers whose terms began December 19, 1887, were commissioners, Charles Werner, J.A. Harris, T.A. Wall; sheriff, George Steell; treasurer, Arthur E. Dickerman; county clerk and recorder, James W. Matkin; probate judge, Herbert P. Rolfe; assessor, Richard T. Gorham; county attorney, George W. Taylor; superintendent of public instruction, Bessie Ford; coroner, J.H. Fairfield; public administrator, J. W. Stanton.... T.A. Wall failed to qualify as commissioner and E.R. Clingan, a businessman of Belt, was appointed to fill the place.*[33]

HOME OF CITY GOVERNMENT

Great Falls was incorporated as a second-class city on October 4, 1888. Paris Gibson was the first mayor, and the council chambers were in the Minot Block. After city elections on November 10, the first city council met on November 21 to hear the first message from newly elected Mayor Paris Gibson. In his message, Mayor Gibson emphasized low taxes, fire protection and the value of trees and parks. City aldermen included the following: First Ward: Dr. Fairfield and R.R. Hotchkiss; Second: Charles Wegner and D.R. Mitchell; Third: J.C. Johnson and J. Matthews; and Fourth: W.P. Beachley and C.N. Dickinson.[34]

HOME OF THE TOWNSITE COMPANY

James J. Hill and Paris Gibson organized the Great Falls Water-Power and Townsite Company in 1887 to develop the town of Great Falls, providing it with power, sewage and water and attracting commerce and industry. In mid-January 1888, the Townsite Company moved into its showcase new quarters on the east side of the ground floor of the Minot building. The counters were made of black birch elegantly finished by E.V. Rubottom; the floors were oiled, with everything neatly arranged. The company occupied three offices: Paris Gibson was ensconced in the front office, and the others were occupied by the secretary and treasurer, respectively.[35]

During the early years, the third floor of Minot Block became a community center for a wide range of activities, as evident in the following sampling. In February 1888, the African American community met at Minot Hall to hear Miss Mary Hutton sing. "All went smoothly for a while but finally the audience became so enthusiastic and noisy that the programme was cut short."[36] In June, the Grand Army of the Republic presented a photo representation of the Battle of Gettysburg in the hall. In December, a company from the Twenty-Fifth Infantry, an African American regiment from Fort Shaw, presented the Fort Shaw Minstrels in a grand performance before a good crowd in the hall.[37]

Political rallies filled Minot Hall during the last years of the 1880s as Montana finally achieved statehood. The Republicans selected their ticket in the hall for the fall 1889 election. In July 1890, the hall was packed with "a large and enthusiastic crowd of workingmen composed of all nationalities" to hear P.F. Boland, a labor organizer for Montana, and J. Zimmerman, a local leader who spoke about a change in position regarding strikes. Whereas in the past, strikes always seemed to involve loss of life and property, leadership was shifting to advocate a peaceful way by arbitration. A second meeting followed the next night to allow other workers to attend and to complete an organization.[38]

In September, the Democrats met in the hall to elect their delegates to the Cascade County Democratic Convention.[39] One week later, the Republicans met in the hall to organize a permanent Republican club.[40] In early October the "colored Republicans" met in Minot Hall for two nights to organize a club.[41]

During the busy month of October, businessmen met to organize and consider the strike situation.[42] Ladies interested in the organization of a Woman's Christian Temperance Union (WCTU) met and chose temporary officers after hearing a temperance lecture; about nineteen ladies signed a pledge to abstain from alcohol.[43]

ELECTRIC CITY CLUB

In the autumn of 1894, Great Falls leaders and businessmen agreed to form a men's club for literary, educational and social purposes. The Electric City Club was incorporated, and quarters were prepared by remodeling the second floor of the Minot Block.[44] The new club rooms opened on December 1, 1894, for a city membership of fifty-seven and ten out-of-town members. The Electric City club filled an important need by furnishing a cozy and comfortable place for city leaders and businessmen to meet and to entertain important visitors.[45] With the leader of the African American community, Edward Simms, serving as steward, the Electric City Club became a social and civic institution for the community for many years.[46]

FROM GLORY TO DEMOLITION

In its early years, the Minot Block assumed the mantle of the "Central Block." It was important to the community as the seat of both Cascade County government (for five years) and the city government and as the home of the First National Bank, a popular meeting hall and the Electric City Club. The First National Bank moved when it built its own bank building; it was replaced by the Cascade Bank. The county offices moved to a new courthouse in 1891. Over the years, businesses came and moved on, and the Central Block's glory days faded. By the 1950s, the B&B Pawn Shop occupied the old bank quarters, while the Town Baths were in the old townsite office. By then, the ancient buildings in the block were being condemned as a "haven for vagrants and drunks." In the fall of 1985, the Minot Block and the rest of the historic buildings sharing the 201 Block on the north side of Central Avenue were lost to history; the wrecking ball of demolition struck with a vengeance, without regard for their storied past.[47]

Chapter 5

RAINBOW CLUB

In mid-June 1889, five-year-old Great Falls had its first men's social club, the Rainbow Club. The *Tribune* announced the opening:

> *The Rainbow Club will throw open its doors to the grace and beauty of Great Falls. The adjoining Arion hall will be devoted to dancing while the guests will be free to wander at their own sweet will through the fine apartments, which under the magic skill of the decorators' art are invested with oriental splendor.*
>
> *The club...is the result of a resolution of some public-spirited citizens that Great Falls should have a club for the enjoyment of its own people and the entertainment of strangers....*
>
> *Accommodation was finally found in the Phelps-Maginnis Block, the upper floor of which was quickly transformed into spacious apartments. Entering the club, you find yourself in the hall and cloak room which are adorned with terra cotta paper hangings and are laid with linoleum. From here it is not far to the reception room. Here the walls and ceilings are symphonies in blue and gold that would have delighted the eye of the aesthetic Whistler. The brussels carpet is beautiful in design and corresponds with the walls and furniture. Elegance and comfort are combined in the massive oak furniture of this fine apartment where members and friends may meet in social converse and view the busy streets and handsome residences on the Missouri, as well as the bold bluffs of the broad river which stand as sentinels beside Black Eagle Falls.*

Above: Edward Simms, revered steward at the Rainbow Club and the Electric City Club and a leader in the Black community of Great Falls. *Author collection.*

Opposite: Elizabeth Simms, Edward's wife and leader of the women in the Union Bethel African Methodist Episcopal Church. *Author collection.*

Adjoining this apartment is the reading room which is accorded a prominent place in all modern clubs. Here the dominant tints are also blue and gold. A spacious table laden with the light and heavy literature of the day invites the searcher for mental recreation to spend some time profitably here. The member finds newspapers and magazines in profusion. It would entail much trouble and expense to collect them at his own home, but here he may browse through them, culling the latest social, sporting, or dramatic news of the day.

Nearby, but separated by a massive wall which dulls the sound are the billiard room and buffet. The billiard tables are simple in design, but they come from a renowned maker which ensures perfection. They rest on a linoleum-covered floor. The walls bear that subdued terra-cotta color which is so pleasing to the eye. There is a flood of light from the windows which look out on Prospect hill and the highlands beside Sun river. Oak chairs and antique design are here in ample number so that, like Falstaff, the club member might say "I will take mine ease in mine inn."

The decoration and furnishing of the club rooms has it may be inferred, been carried out with much success by Messrs. Atkinson, Shur, Dickerman and Howard Crosby who no doubt will be mentally awarded a vote of thanks by the fair assembled there tonight "to chase the glowing hours with nimble feet."

The Rainbow club has now an active membership of over 70. Its president is Franklin P. Atkinson of the Cascade bank, and its vice president is John R. Payne of the Bank of Great Falls, with Howard Crosby as secretary and treasurer.[48]

POPULAR STEWARD EDWARD SIMMS

The Rainbow Club had a festive opening that evening with most members present and Edward Simms, the steward, acting as "master of ceremonies." Simms and his wife, Elizabeth, were the first two African Americans to settle in the new town, in the spring of 1886. Simms had arrived at Fort Benton on the steamboat *Red Cloud* and worked in the dining room of the Choteau House before moving on to Fort Shaw to work as assistant to the post trader Joseph McKnight. In Great Falls, Simms was chef at the Cascade Hotel and then janitor at the Cascade County courthouse in the Minot Block. At the opening of the Rainbow Club, Ed Simms was present as steward, providing food and service to members, which grew rapidly into respect and friendship.[49]

From its opening, the Rainbow Club proved "the very perfection of clubdom."[50]

In August 1889, a grand ball was given in Arion Hall and the parlors of the Rainbow Club in honor of visitors to Great Falls. The informal party given in honor of visiting young ladies featured dancing to the Gibbons Orchestra until eleven o'clock, when the party sat down to

> *a sumptuous supper prepared by Mr. Ed Simms, who did himself credit. Dancing then resumed and continued to a late hour. Many of the young ladies and gentlemen were in formal dress, which added greatly to the beauty of the whole affair.*[51]

MOVING TO BACH-CORY BLOCK

By 1891, the Rainbow Club had moved into the fourth floor of the Bach-Cory Block. In the early spring of 1892, local and invited members of the medical profession gathered for the first annual meeting and banquet of the North Montana District Medical Association at the Rainbow Club.

> *The gentlemen of medicine forgot for the time the ills of life and devoted their thoughts to the consideration of subjects pertaining to the welfare of the profession and incidentally to partaking of the good things prepared by Ed Simms.*[52]

THE END

With the Panic of 1893, featuring a crash in silver prices, Great Falls and Montana went into a depression. Hard times came along, and some banks closed their doors, forcing businessmen to cut down every unnecessary expense. The Rainbow Club, which had once been a very prosperous institution, entered rocky times and, by the late summer of 1893, had been forced to close its doors, much to the regret of many citizens.[53]

Chapter 6

VALERIA LIBRARY

In Great Falls' third year, 1886, when the town had just six hundred residents, editor Will Hanks of the *Tribune* advocated for a fire department, a church and a public library. Methodist minister John Reid and others began canvassing to establish a free library and reading room that fall.[54]

The Manitoba Railroad arrived the next year, and Great Falls commenced serious growth, yet it was not until May 1889 that real action began for a library with a meeting, chaired by Herbert O. Chowen, in the Great Falls Townsite Company office. At that meeting, the Townsite Company promised a lot on Second Avenue North and Third Street, and a committee formed to prepare a development plan and convene an organizational meeting.[55]

During the summer of 1889, committee members Charles M. Webster, Reverend John Reid, Reverend John Reid Jr., *Leader* editor Herbert P. Rolfe, Mrs. Dr. Alfred G. Ladd and teacher Miss Jesse Rich prepared plans for a private, not public, library. Herbert Chowen met Valeria Gibson, wife of founder Paris, at the Gibson home in Minneapolis and received her promise to donate a collection of books from her friends. Paris Gibson donated a valuable thirty-nine-volume *Works of Hubert Howe Bancroft*, while O.C. Mortson donated the "pride" of the collection, the *Encyclopedia Britannica*. As plans for the Valeria Art and Library Association matured in the fall of 1889, the townsite donated the lot ($4,000), and building fundraising began. Shares cost $5 each, and fundraising was led by Paris Gibson ($500), Robert Vaughn and H.O. Chowen ($250 each) and others who purchased from one to twenty-five shares. Later, the Townsite Company donated a second adjoining lot on the corner of Second Avenue North and Third Street—the site of the future Carnegie Library in 1903 and today's Great Falls Public Library in 1967.[56]

Library plans were spurred on by public sentiment among the rapidly growing population. Many of the new residents were young single men, and one of them expressed the need for a library well in his letter to the editor in the *Tribune*:

> *Now that the winter months are at hand and the nights are cool some place of resort should be provided for the young men of the city that will be free from the temptations of city life....Many young men are living in rooms which have no conveniences for fire, and they must spend their evenings and leisure hours somewhere. Let us have a reading room and public library. Signed "One of the Young Men."*[57]

By mid-December 1889, the Valeria Art and Library Association, then with 450 volumes, found a temporary home over the tailor shop of William Nalbach at 211 Central Avenue. Trustees Herbert O. Chowen, Mrs. Alfred G. Ladd, Theodore Gibson, Herbert P. Rolfe, William M. Cockrill, Daniel L. Tracy and Edgar G. Maclay organized the library, drafted its bylaws and constitution and prepared to open to subscribers.[58]

On January 20, 1890, librarian Robert Williams opened the doors of the Valeria Library, located in the Milner and Boardman Block on Second Street North. The library offered two rooms to patrons, who paid one dollar per month, and was open every day from one to five o'clock in the afternoon and from seven to ten o'clock in the evening. Art exhibits and concerts were held by local talent as well as visiting groups, such as the Mendelssohn Quintet of Boston.[59]

In October 1890, Hunt and Holscher completed architectural plans for the Valeria Library building, and contracts were let to Buckingham and Olsen for $1,355; to G.H. Graham for cut stone work ($98); and to McKay Brothers for brickwork ("common," $625, and "pressed brick facing," $700). The plans provided for a building with a foundation and trimmings of brown cut stone from the Ulm quarry and walls of pressed brick.[60]

Located on Third Street North, between Second and Third Avenues, the new Valeria Library stood one story in height and was divided into four rooms. The entrance opened onto a cozy vestibule and the librarian's room. A hallway led to the main reading room, which was sixteen by thirty-three feet. Connected to the larger reading room by folding doors was a smaller

Valeria Library, named for the wife of Paris Gibson, opened in 1890 and became a free city public library in 1892. *Author collection.*

room for private study, about half the size of the first, and a broad alcove with bookshelves. A basement beneath contained a furnace. The rooms were all well lit by windows, those in front having neat colored transoms of cut glass. Today, this cut glass is displayed in the Montana Room of the Great Falls Public Library.[61]

Construction began in late November 1890 and proceeded rapidly through the winter to completion at a cost of $5,000. When the new Valeria Library formally opened on Monday, March 9, 1891, a major art exhibition was held for the benefit of the library fund. The exhibition featured several hundred etchings and watercolors by modern artists obtained from New York especially for the occasion. Artistically and financially, the exhibition was a success, drawing large crowds and many buyers. Impromptu musical entertainment and hot tea each evening added to the festive occasion.[62]

The Valeria Library was off to a good start, with highly educated botanist Robert Williams serving as librarian and a stock of about eight hundred history, fiction and reference works together with the latest newspapers, magazines and periodicals. The reading rooms were open to the public

Valeria Library's first librarian was the highly educated botanist Robert Williams, shown here in his office. *Author collection.*

without charge (the young men were no doubt pleased to find an evening home), while to check out books, the nominal cost was fifty cents per month. Library officers were H.O. Chowen, president; Theodore Gibson, treasurer; and Robert Williams, secretary and librarian. Mrs. Dr. Ladd, J.S. Tod, E.G. Maclay and Frank B. Wilcox served as directors. After one year, Williams left Great Falls, and Miss Eloise Petit (later Mrs. Mayor Charles M. Webster) was appointed librarian.[63]

In April 1892, the City of Great Falls took over the library (land, building and books), and it became the Valeria Public Library. Any resident of Great Falls could borrow books without charge. A city ordinance passed on April 4, 1892, read in part, "Ladies over the age of twenty-one shall be eligible to the office of director of said library." Lutie E. Weitman was selected as librarian.[64]

In 1962, the seventy-year-old Valeria Library was demolished. *From the* Tribune, *September 22, 1962.*

By 1896, Bella Brown was serving as librarian, and recent high school graduate Mabel Collins became her assistant. The Valeria Library served well during the early years of Great Falls as the cultural and literary center of the town. The city experienced explosive growth during the 1890s, and by the end of the century, the little library was overwhelmed. It ceased operation in 1903, replaced by a larger library funded by Andrew Carnegie.[65]

The beautiful little Valeria building had several lives over the almost six decades that followed. It became the first home of the YWCA in 1911, and after World War I, veterans organized a Soldiers' and Sailors' Club there that became the American Legion. By 1920, the building had become known as Veterans Hall, and it served veterans from the Grand Army of the Republic, the Spanish-American War and the American Legion and its auxiliaries. Later, some public school classes met in its rooms, and during World War II, it was the home of the Victory Book program, sending books to servicemen overseas. Library books were stored in the Valeria until 1956, when use of the building was discontinued.[66]

In 1962, Valeria Library was demolished, clearing the way for Library Park. Today, this first cultural center in Great Falls is remembered through photographs displayed in the Great Falls Public Library and the beautiful stained-glass windows hanging in the Montana Room. The Valeria Library began the tradition of exceptional library service to the Great Falls community.[67]

Chapter 7

GREAT FALLS & CANADA RAILWAY

The arrival of the first coal cars at the depot in Westside Great Falls late in the evening on October 2, 1890, heralded the dawn of a new era. Fort Benton, long the origin of steamboat trade and shared heritage with western Canada along the famed Whoop-Up Trail, was being replaced by Great Falls. In just its sixth year, the "future great," Great Falls, with electricity from Black Eagle Dam and new industrial copper works, was ready to boom, and the new international railroad would bring coal from the Galt mines near Lethbridge. The narrow-gauge track of the new railroad, popularly known as the Turkey Trail, followed much of the path of the old Whoop-Up Trail.[68]

By February 1890, Donald Grant and I.M. Ross, the contractors building the Turkey Trail, had two surveying parties in the field and carpenters at work building an engineering corps headquarters near the stockyards located just west of today's Jack Club Mall in Great Falls. Plans were in place for a large freight and storage warehouse, 150 × 30 feet, where all the supplies for the construction corps of the new road would be stored. Over the coming eight months, the 134-mile narrow-gauge track would be laid to the international border, passing along the Sun River to Sunnyside (today's Vaughn), then north up Muddy Creek to the upper Teton, proceeding fourteen miles up the Dry Fork of the Marias, crossing the river near Fort Conrad and touching west of the Sweet Grass Hills to cross the border at Coutts. There, it would connect to the final sixty-six-mile line of the Alberta Railroad and Coal Company to continue to the great Galt coal fields and the town of Lethbridge.[69]

This narrow-gauge engine was the first engine to operate on the Great Falls to Lethbridge Railroad. *From the* Tribune, *May 26, 1963.*

Sir Alexander T. Galt, a Montreal-based Canadian businessman and politician, and his son, Elliott, were the powers behind the coal company and the rail lines. On October 3, 1889, Galt incorporated the Great Falls & Canada Railroad in Montana while, at that time, the Alberta Railroad and Coal Co. line was building south to Coutts.[70]

The Turkey Trail passed through northern Montana country potentially rich in agriculture and minerals, to open that developing region to the markets of the world. While it didn't last long and its short life was beset with trouble, the little narrow-gauge rail line played an important role in developing this northern region.

By April 1890, about five hundred men were at work building the new line with two engines and thirty cars in support, laying three to four miles of track per day. The ties were secured from the head of the Sun River Valley. According to a study by Duane A. Olson of Great Falls,

> *The laborers of the road got only $1.50 for a 10-hour day. The line was 134.37 miles long with five miles of siding. The rail was 35 pound per yard steel. The roadbed was narrow, and the line had light timber bridges with Howe truss spans at the crossings of the Marias and Teton rivers. The grades were up to 1.25 percent and the curvatures up to 10 degrees.*
>
> **Completed**
>
> *The railroad was completed Oct. 1, 1890. The coal trestle at Great Falls for transferring coal to standard gauge cars, was 1,000 feet long and 36 feet high. About 15 to 20 standard gauge cars could be filled at once.*

Starting on Oct. 20, special trains for a week's excursion were leaving Great Falls daily. Roundtrip tickets were $10 from Great Falls to Lethbridge.... The trains left Great Falls at 8 a.m. and arrived at Lethbridge at 5 p.m. About 200 miles of grading and track work had been completed in 106 days.

The first coal train left Lethbridge Oct. 2, 1890. In Lethbridge the price of lots skyrocketed when plans were made for the north and south railroad. Many new buildings sprang up when the railroad finally reached here.

In Great Falls, a big banquet was given at the Hotel Bristol by Phil Gibson in honor of Donald Grant and other Great Falls and Canada officials.

At the line's first annual meeting in 1891 Sir A.T. Galt was named president and T.E. Collins [of Great Falls], *vice president.*[71]

BESET BY TROUBLE

Almost from the beginning, trouble for the Great Falls & Canada came in many forms, not least being the opposition of the Great Northern Railroad of James J. Hill, which was striving for a monopoly on rail service in northern Montana. Injuries led to contract labor suits, there were charges of smuggling coal across the border and a massive Marias range prairie fire was rumored to have been started by a sparks from a Great Falls & Canada train.

Yet the five hundred to one thousand tons of Galt coal arriving in Great Falls each day kept the line operating. That coal fueled the new copper works in Great Falls as well as copper operations in Butte. A new Great Falls depot was planned for a site close to the west bank of the Missouri with better access to the Boston and Montana Smelter. In 1894, a new line to Bynum was proposed, and in Duane Olson's words:

Everything looked beautiful in 1894 on the Great Falls and Canada except the budget. The net profit for the year was $6,619, which was hardly enough for any big expansion program.... The net profit for the year of 1895 dropped to $1,269.[72]

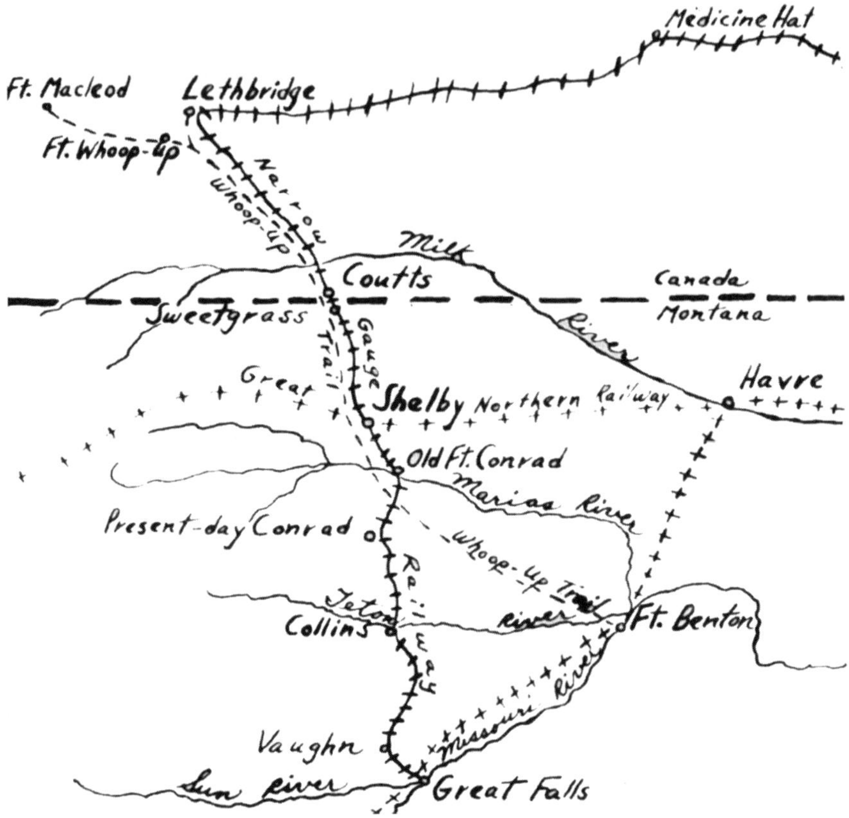

The route of the "Turkey Trail" railroad from Great Falls to Lethbridge through north central Montana and on to Alberta, Canada. *From the* Tribune, *May 26, 1963.*

THE GREAT CREE DEPORTATION

In early 1896, Congress passed the Cree Deportation Act, providing for the expulsion of the Indigenous Cree from the United States, back to their homelands in western Canada. Historian and folklorist Nicholas Vrooman summarized this action, which was centered on Great Falls, in these words:

> *But before the ink was dry from signing the Cree Deportation Act, the U.S. Army out of Fort Assiniboine, near Havre, mobilized. Beginning in June, and completing their task in August, a full complement of Buffalo Soldier cavalry, led by a young Lt. John J. Pershing, shipped in cattle cars, or*

> *herded well over 500 "Crees" to Alberta, Canada. They were dispatched to reserves throughout the province. Many immediately snuck back across the border into Montana and hid out....*
>
> *Most of the deported Montana "Cree" made it back to* [Montana], *hiding out in the coulees, draws, and canyons, mixing in with relatives on reservations, or continuing to press their luck around their old haunts, camping at the dumps, continuing in their community strategy, living in the Moccasin Flat, Buckskin Flat, and Breedtown refugee camps around the state, getting pick-up work on the ranches of the Hi-Line and scavenging in the dumps of the cities.*[73]

The *Great Falls Leader* editorialized after the first major "human cargo" shipment of Crees on the Great Falls & Canada:

> ***Crees Have Gone***
>
> *Rather Than Leave Great Falls, Raining Bow Takes His Life*
>
> *The Crees have gone. The plot of ground across the river which for two months past have been their home is vacant and but one of their number remains in Great Falls. He will be buried today by the county. The balance of the party left yesterday at 11:45 for a new hunting ground on Canadian soil and at 9 o'clock this morning arrived at their destination....*
>
> *Yesterday morning officers were busy at 5 o'clock at the camp. The evening previous Lieut. Wilder with a detachment of men arrived from Fort Assinniboine to escort the Indians to the border. The order to pack up and move was given by Maj. Sanno on the arrival of Lieut. Wilder and by 11 o'clock 86 Crees, 180 horses and all the equipments of the camp were loaded on the train. Three-quarters of an hour later the train pulled out of the Great Falls & Canada depot in two sections and was run through without stopping.*
>
> *The proceedings were not without the mar of excitement. About 9 o'clock Raining Bow or Rain of the Bow, an Indian 40 years of age, approached the commanding officer and told him that as they were leaving for Canada, he wanted a big paper to protect him on his arrival there. After asking for it several times it was promised him, and Lieut. Pershing supposed he was satisfied. Fifteen minutes later he was surprised at his work by hearing the report of a rifle. Raining Bow had suicided. After leaving the lieutenant he went to his tent, where he had a 45 Winchester rifle. Taking this in his hand he walked outside and called several of the Indians about him. After a short consultation he raised the rifle and, placing it to his breast,*

pulled the trigger. The bullet entered just below the heart. Dr. Ferguson was summoned, and the dying Indian was removed to the Columbus hospital, where he died last night. Being a good Indian, he was this morning buried by the county. Raining Bow had determined not to go back to Canada unless he was granted a free pardon for past offenses. According to the reasons given by Buffalo Coat he was under a Canadian indictment from a Canadian jury for murder in the first degree and had been informed of that fact. He participated in the Duck Lake massacre and later in the murder of three priests at a mission some miles from Duck Lake, and rather than surrender he concluded to die....

Today or tomorrow about fifty more Crees will arrive here from Billings and will be shipped at once.[74]

COAL MARKET LOST

By May 1896, local Sand Coulee coal mines had gone into full production, delivering coal to Great Falls for half the price of Galt coal. Rumors of a change to standard gauge remained just that. At the time, the net earnings of the line were $14,212. Equipment included seven engines, two passenger cars, an express car and 157 freight cars; five more passenger cars were acquired over the next two years. A daily train now ran to Shelby, near the Canadian border.[75]

Early in 1901, president of the line Sir A.T. Galt made a formal application to the Dominion Parliament of Canada for permission to lease the line's railroad property in Canada and the United States to the Canadian Pacific. Opposition from the Great Northern kept the Canadian Pacific out of Great Falls. Just months later, the Montana and Great Northern Railroad was incorporated to purchase the Great Falls & Canada for $750,000. The Montana and Great Northern was a subsidiary of the Great Northern Railroad.[76]

THE END OF THE TURKEY TRAIL

The end was nearing for the Turkey Trail. The new Montana and Great Northern enabled the Great Northern to attain a monopoly over all competition in northern Montana.[77] In his study, Duane Olson summed up the last years of the Great Falls & Canada:

> *The Great Northern was not to assume control until the gauge was standardized. Before Oct. 30, 1902, according to the deed, the Great Falls and Canada was to have widened the gauge, thereby ending the life of the narrow gauge. While the line was being widened, business was carried on as usual by the process of adding a third rail.*[78]

On January 3, 1903, the saga of the Turkey Trail came to an end when the last train pulled out from the Westside depot. A *Leader* reporter was on scene:

The Passing of the "Turkey Trail" Road

"Last call for the Great Falls & Canada. All aboard." Conductor Jack Howard waved his hand at Engineer Jack Kain sitting in the little peekaboo cab of Engine No. 6, and with much wheezing and puffing, the last train ever to pass over the Great Falls & Canada railway, pulled out from the Westside depot at 3:05 this afternoon....

The last "Turkey Trail" train leaving the station at Great Falls. *From the* Great Falls Leader *(hereafter* Leader*), January 3, 1903.*

The crew today which closed the story for the Great Falls & Canada were Jack Howard, conductor; J. Kain, engineer; Andy Nevin, fireman; Frank Davies and Orr McIlmoyle, brakemen. The train was drawn by engine No. 6, and there were eight empties, three coal loads, one caboose, one baggage car, one passenger coach and switch engine No. 1.

There were but a few on hand to view the passing of the narrow gauge, and Agent Fowler told stories over the wire to the agent at Lethbridge while waiting for the final act.

Ballentyne to the Rescue

Just when hope had almost faded Alex Ballentyne, the Teton county sheepman, drifted into the room and Mr. Fowler dashed at him like a cyclone.

"Do you want a ticket": he asked, and Mr. Ballentyne remarked that he did as far as Collins.

"That," remarked Mr. Fowler, with a sigh of relief, "is two dollars and fifteen cents, and we have a cash passenger for the last train which will ever run over the Great Falls & Canada." Mr. Ballentyne planked down the $2.15, and Mr. Fowler slammed down the little cage window upon the traffic business of the Great Falls & Canada forever.

Mr. Fowler had a personal interest in the matter of taking Mr. Ballentyne's dough, as he took the first cash fare ever sold over the line out of Lethbridge in October 1890, and has been with the road ever since, and as the little train went puffing and wheezing over the little bumpy rails Mr. Fowler looked sorry.

Was Pioneer Upbuilder

The little turkey trail which went out today is the last narrow gauge left in the west, and in its time did much toward the upbuilding of northern Montana. It was finished between this city and Lethbridge October 3, 1890, and was built to haul the coal from Lethbridge mines to this city; a job at which the little road has been pounding away ever since. Sometimes the trains were a few days later, at other times there were floods which wiped it out, and occasionally the wind blew trains off the track, but always there was something doing and the little road aided Great Falls greatly in her upbuilding. One year ago, the line was sold to the Great Northern and the gauge has been broadened and Monday morning [January 5] *the Montana and Great Northern will begin operations between this city and the Canadian line….*

There will never again be anything doing on the Great Falls & Canada, and the annals of the turkey trail have passed into history.[79]

Chapter 8

STREET RAILWAY COMPANY

The Great Falls Street Railway Company commenced operations on July 1, 1890, with streetcars drawn by horses. By the end of July, a "dinkey" steam-powered "motor" had begun operation. In the words of the *Leader*, "It had in tow one open coach and the two glided along as gracefully as a young maiden with a new silk dress."[80] One month later, a reporter for the *Tribune* tried out the new transportation line, observing the remarkable growth of the new city, then just six years old, along the way.

Great Falls Is Going Ahead
Signs of Advancement on Every Side—A Trip Over the Motor Line
Work at the Great Dam and Smelter
A Power Station Built Near the Black Eagle Falls—A Powerful Dynamo

Taking the motor at the Park hotel the traveler soon finds himself on the southside amid new houses that have all sprung up this spring. On turning the corner at Sixth avenue, some temporary structures appear which ought to give place to something more comfortable before winter comes. In building, the southside holds its own. It will benefit by the motor which enables people to do shopping up town and return without much delay. It is surprising how far ten minutes' ride on the cars will take people in the residence districts. This ensures the rapid settlement of the southside to Prospect Hill and perhaps beyond.

An early steam-powered streetcar with a small engine pulling an open-sided passenger car. *THM*.

> *Above south Ninth street the buildings are scattered. The new street sign boards are useful here, for the oldest inhabitant might be puzzled to tell the locations. But this part of the city is in a fair way to thrive rapidly. It is remote enough from the railroad, business, and manufacturing districts to be regarded with favor for elegant homes.*
>
> *It is when the motor turns into north Fifteenth street that this year's growth is most apparent. It is not long ago since Alderman Burghardt appeared to be going into the wilderness when he built so far out on the north side. Now there are houses all around him and more are going up. Between Fourth avenue north and the river are fine residences of which any town might be proud. Those of R.R. Hotchkiss and Theo. Gibson are notable. Sheriff Hamilton has a fine brick house in this locality and so has Mr.*

> *Paul. The noble symmetrical school house seems in fact the center around which many happy homes are grouped, which is quite proper. The north side has all the churches except the Presbyterian. The Catholic church is the largest of all and yet it seems none too large for the present congregation not to speak of that may be expected before long.*
>
> *The motor passes through thriving districts all the way, but it is at the end of the line that progress seems to begin. The power station is now provided with a large boiler, a powerful engine built by Armington & Sims, of Providence, R.I., and a dynamo of great capacity from the Thomson-Houston Co. of Lynn, Mass. Another large building will be erected nearby for machinery. Pipes are being laid to the river in order to draw a plentiful supply of water therefrom.…In the distance the smoke of the Silver smelter proclaims that the industrial limits of Great Falls extend far beyond even the Black Eagle Falls.*[81]

Just seven months later, on March 17, 1891, the Street Railway rolled out the first cars run by electricity, enabled by the completion of the Black Eagle Dam and the electricity generated. Superintendent Dickinson of the Great Falls Street Railway company announced this step forward, saying:

> *This will improve our streetcar service a little, for as soon as the electricity is applied, we intend to make ten trips daily instead of six, as at present. We are adding to our power facilities, but yet we find them totally inadequate to meet the pressing demand of the company. We have been obliged to put in a new engine and boiler and other expensive improvements so as to tide the company over till the immense waterpower of the Missouri can be utilized. Then we purpose furnishing a service that will shut out any possible chance for competition.*[82]

SERVING WELL

Over the next forty years, the street railway served the Great Falls community well, expanding to 18.67 miles of track to reach all parts of the growing city with two sets of cars: an open car set for summer and a closed car set for winter.

By 1931, automobiles and trucks were dominating transportation, and buses were replacing streetcars. The railway, by then owned by the Montana

Streetcars on Central Avenue at Fourth Street looking east. *Author collection.*

Power Company, decided to end its entire operation. The district manager of Montana Power, Frank Scotten, ended the service with a couple of funeral parties for the streetcars.

END OF AN ERA

On Tuesday, November 24, Lions Club members led by Scotten boarded a chartered streetcar at Park Drive for a final ride, hearing a sketch of the railway's history since operations started in 1890. The *Tribune* reported on this nostalgic ride:

> ***Scotten Traces Street Car History at Lions Program***
> ***Club Has Lunch on Chartered Car as Farewell Gesture to System Which Will Be Replaced Soon by Busses***
>
> *Observing the passing of the street railway system in Great Falls and the advent of bus service here, members of the Lions club Tuesday rode and ate lunch in a chartered street car and heard a sketch of the railway's activities since operation started in 1890, given by Frank Scotten, manager of the Montana Power company. Earl Burgett presided.*
>
> *The club members boarded the car at Park drive and Central avenue and rode to a siding at Fourth avenue north and Thirty-sixth street where the program was held. A large banner on the side of the car bade farewell to it and pointed a welcoming arrow to the bus system, represented by an Austin, driven immediately at the rear.*
>
> *S.S. Hawks, superintendent of the street railway, was introduced as part of the program.*
>
> *In tracing the early history of the street railway, Mr. Scotten said the old-type Burney four-wheel cars were used here and they carried about 20 people. Two men formed the crew, and they worked a 10-hour shift for a daily wage of $2.25. Labor costs recently have been higher with one-man cars.*
>
> ***Franchise in 1889***
>
> *The first franchise for operation of street cars was granted by the city council in 1889. Operation began in 1890 and at that time one car was in use here, drawn by a "dinkey" steam locomotive. Electric car operations*

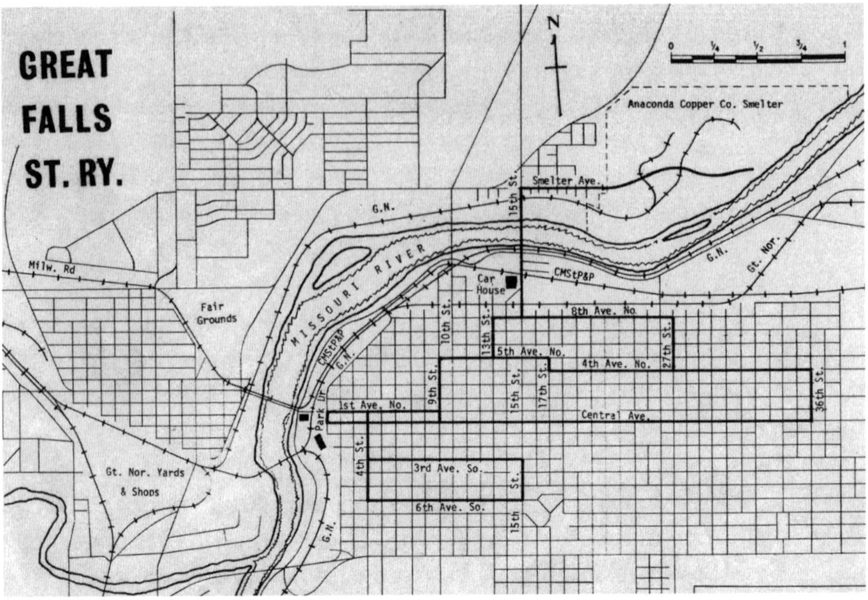

Great Falls streetcar map. *THM.*

began in 1891. Two other franchises have been granted to the railway since then, one in 1905 and another in 1927.

Mr. Scotten referred to the old days "when the fare was a nickel and it looked as big as quarter does now." There are several employees with the company who have worked since it began operations, 42 years ago.

For a time, the railway had competition. In 1892 a franchise was granted to another operator here. His line ran on First avenue north from Park drive to Ninth street. There was one car, one trip a day was made, and the car was drawn by one mule. The line ran about a year before it was absorbed.

Mr. Scotten noted that there had been a general falling off in the street railway business of the United States.... The same trend has been seen here, Mr. Scotten said. Along about the year 1920, the average number of passengers carried daily was 12,000. The average now is 2,000. The largest number ever carried here was on circus day in August 1923, when there were 20,980.

Many Extra Trips

Ten years ago, an average of 3,000 passengers were being carried on the smelter line alone, Mr. Scotten said, and 38 extra trips were made daily to accommodate them. The increase in the number of private automobiles is accepted as the major reason for the reduction of passengers....

The local railway owns 27 street cars, some of which have run more than 700,000 miles. The present cars were put in use in 1911. There are 18.6 miles of track in Great Falls.

Mr. Scotten also pointed to the improved accident record of the line here. In 1926 there were 273 accidents of all kinds, including derailments, collisions, and mishaps on the cars. For the first 10 months of the present year 43 have been recorded.[83]

END OF AN ERA

The streetcar era ended at midnight on November 30, 1931, as Scotten gathered guests at the Rainbow Hotel for a wake. They passed by a bier on which a battered streetcar lay. Music began as the guests boarded a streetcar for a midnight funeral ride to travel over the Boston Heights Route to the city's eastern end.

The end of the era brought forth memories of old-time street railway employees. Charles A. Hillstrand began working for the company before cars were running. On May 28, 1890, he was engaged by contractor Hugh Kirkendall to help grade the first track. Hillstrand retired from active service in 1926, after thirty-six years' service.

FIRST GIRL ON CAR

Hillstrand recalled that the first girl to ride on a streetcar in Great Falls was Arvonia, the daughter of Robert Vaughn, legendary pioneer. In 1931, Arvonia, then Mrs. H.M. Sprague, did not remember having this experience as a young child but recalled her father relating the story. One afternoon, Sam Wilber, Great Falls transfer man, hitched a span of horses to one of the cars. Frank Donovan was the conductor on the car, and Vaughn and his baby daughter boarded as passengers.

The first line Hillstrand recalled ran up Central Avenue from Park Drive to Second Street. It then turned south to Sixth Avenue and ran up Sixth Avenue to Ninth Street, from where it turned north to Fifth Avenue North.

Tracks went up Fifth Avenue to Thirteenth Street, north to Eighth Avenue and then on to Black Eagle Park. The line was four miles long.[84]

Images of streetcars on the streets of Great Falls seem apocryphal today, yet streetcars ran along lines the length of Great Falls for four decades, providing essential transit around the growing city before the advent of automobiles and buses.

Chapter 9

VOLK BREWERY

Volk Brewery was the original brewing plant in Great Falls. Located on Upper River Road south of Great Falls in Great Falls Park (today's Verde Park), Nicholas and Christian Volk opened their brewery in 1891. Their brewery wagons delivered beer to workers throughout the region. The upper portion of the brewery, built of wood and stone, burned to the ground in 1894.

VOLK BROTHERS PIONEERED IN BREWING INDUSTRY

During the first years of the Great Falls Townsite, thirsty residents quenched their palates with beer from breweries at Sun River, Fort Benton and Helena, as well as beer shipped in from St. Louis. Nicholas and Christian Volk, whose father, Carl, operated a brewery in Alexandria, Minnesota, arrived in Great Falls in 1888 determined to bring fine-quality brews to the new town. The brothers paid $275 an acre for land on the south side of Prospect Hill, about a mile south of the new town. In October 1889, the first talk of a local brewery in Great Falls began, and by June 1890, work was well underway building the Volk Bros. Brewery. Construction used stone quarried at the site and brick made from firm clay nearby.[85]

Five months later, in late October 1890, the *Leader* reported on progress:

> *The new brewery being run by Volk Bros. situated on the south side of town, is fast nearing completion. They have already finished the brewery kettle, which has been built by Mr. John Meier, bricklayer, and furnace builder at the old* [silver] *smelter, and finished in a thoroughly workmanlike manner, and before long there will be a good supply of beer for the city.*[86]

VOLK BROS. BREWERY

By Christmas 1890, the new brewery had begun brewing Volk Beer of excellent quality and flavor. The Christmas edition of the *Tribune* covered developments:

> *The new brewery of the Volk Bros. is nearly complete. It is situated in the southern part of town about one-fourth of a mile from the city water works. The brewery building is constructed of wood and stone combined and is substantially built in every respect. It is two stories high and is 125 feet long by thirty-five feet in width. On the first floor is a room forty by thirty-five feet. This room is used for boiling the beer, which is done in an immense copper kettle capable of holding twenty barrels. Beyond the boiling room on the same floor are the cellars in which the fresh beer is stored away in large*

Opposite: Volk Bros. Brewery, Great Falls' first brewery, opened in 1891 in Great Falls Park. *THM.*

Above: The Volk home adjacent to the brewery. *THM.*

vats to get age and be ready for use. These two cellars are eighty-five by thirty-five feet in size and have a storage capacity of 800 barrels.

In the second story is the water tank, cooling floor and the ice houses. The brewery has a capacity to turn out twenty barrels daily and it will start up in full force about the 8th of January 1891. It will give employment to nine men at the start and this force will be added to as the business increases.

The Volk Bros. have already brewed several times and have quite a quantity of beer on hand, which is of a very fine quality and has an excellent flavor very similar to the famous Milwaukee beer. The owners are practical brewers and have had years of experience in the famous breweries of Milwaukee. They will no doubt soon work up a large trade.[87]

GREAT FALLS PARK AT THE BREWERY

With the Volk Brewery off to a good beginning, the brothers broadened their operation to form an adjacent amusement park along the Missouri

River and its popular steamboat excursions. In the spring of 1893, Great Falls Park began advertising itself as "a delightful summer resort."

> *Great Falls Park at the Brewery—A Delightful Summer Resort. Beautiful shade trees and outdoor games of all kinds. One mile and a half up the river by steamboat. Swings and other amusements for the young people. Dances twice a week, Wednesdays, and Sundays. The park will be let to clubs, societies, or other organizations at reasonable rates. Volk Bros., Props.*[88]
>
> *To those who desire to not ride so far or may choose the Great Falls park at Volk Bros.' brewery are offered pleasures, which are to be found in few other locations, by this enterprising firm.*
>
> *Great Falls park is one and one-half miles by river above the* [Broadwater Bay] *boathouse and, although just laid out is meeting with well-deserved success. It is laid out on a symmetrical plan, evergreens planted in profusion, giving a good shade, and scenting the air with the fragrance of pine. Surrounding the large pavilion, in which there is a look-out tower also, are many octagonal summer houses and the inner man is provided for at a lunch counter. All kinds of drinks may be obtained, including the beer made at the brewery near-by.*[89]

The combination of Great Falls Park and Volk Brewery beer proved popular with the public. The park was outfitted with a beer garden, a dance pavilion and gazebos. Many social groups picnicked and enjoyed outings at the park, no doubt consuming Volk Beer in quantities. Groups like the local Turnverein brought large crowds to the park, where they enjoyed sports and games while relaxing under the shade of pine trees. After parading through Great Falls, the seventeen members of the Sand Coulee Brass Band picnicked at the park, providing dance music throughout the afternoon and evening. The Guard Christopher Columbus brought the Boston and Montana Band to the park for their first annual ball. Many other groups, large and small, enjoyed excursions to the park.[90]

On July 4, 1894, the small steamboats *J.J. Hill* and *Minnie* plied the river all day and late into the night carrying hundreds of passengers to and from Park Island and Great Falls Park, taking regular trips from the wharf every thirty minutes. Herring Bros. had fitted up the park at Volk Brewery for a ball to be held in the evening. Olson and Race's orchestra played, the dance drew a large crowd and "a good time [was] had by the participants." Advertising emphasized that the dance "will be of the highest class and none need be afraid to take their wives, daughters and sweethearts."[91]

VOLK BREWERY DESTROYED BY FIRE

Tragedy struck at one o'clock in the morning on October 22, 1894, when a fire broke out in the Volk Brewery, and before it was discovered, the building was entirely enveloped in flames, which rose far above Prospect Hill. Two hours later, the entire brewery and the storage house, which contained five hundred barrels of beer and ten barrels of whiskey, were a mass of smoldering ruins. Just one building belonging to the brewery proper was saved: a frame icehouse, located across an alley about ten feet from the storage house. The value of the plant that burned was about $30,000; just over half of that was insured.

The origin of the fire is a mystery; it may have started in the roof over the engine room. Rumors of arson remained unproven.

The Volk brothers lived in a stone house within fifty feet of the plant. When Christian Volk awakened, his bedroom was lit by the flames. He sprang out of bed, dressed and rushed out. In the engine room, a watchman known as Frenchy slept. Volk ran to the engine room door and kicked it open. The roof above had been burned away, and the room was dense with smoke. Volk dragged Frenchy out through the flames, saving his life. Nothing could be saved at the brewery or the storehouse. The flames spread to the icehouse but were put out with water.

The lower story of the brewery was brick and stone and the upper part frame. Only scrap iron remained of the machinery, as well as a portion of the stone wall.

After operating for four glorious years, Volk Brewery was gone. By then, several other larger breweries had begun operating on the Great Falls scene. While the brothers intended to rebuild their brewery, they never did. The city would wait four decades for a new brewery, until 1935, when Christian's sons opened the Volk Brewery in the city at Fourth Street South.[92]

Despite the tragic end of the Volk Brewery, the Volks continued to live at Great Falls Park until about 1910, and the park continued sporadic operations until 1923, when Jack Dempsey leased it to train for the most unlikely heavyweight championship fight ever held.[93]

Chapter 10

GRAND OPERA HOUSE

In a passionate editorial in February 1891, the *Leader* challenged the Great Falls Board of Trade to build an opera house for the six-year-old town, which was beginning to undergo dramatic growth:

> *Everybody believes that Great Falls should have an opera house, and that an almost absolute necessity calls for its erection during the present season. The* Leader *is ready to encourage any enterprise that will supply the need. If the "Board of Procrastination" can do anything to reach the desired end, all good and well, but experience does not teach that much could be accomplished in that way.*[94]

The earliest known photo of the Grand Opera, the cultural gem of Great Falls. The Grand Opera, with its Romanesque décor and spectacular interior, opened in 1891. *THM.*

A stock company was quickly formed, and by April, an opera house seemed assured. Plans were moving forward for a large building on the corner of Third Street and Second Avenue North. In May, the opera house company contracted for plans for a sandstone building by prominent theatrical architect Oscar Cobb, who was well on his way to a stunning career designing some two hundred theaters and opera houses, including the grand opera houses in St. Paul and Minneapolis.[95]

In late June, Oscar Cobb arrived in Great Falls with plans in hand and met a reporter from the *Tribune*, who provided insight into the plans:

Our New Opera House
The House to Be Handsomely Built, Finished, Furnished and Fitted—A Full Description of the Building

Architect Oscar Cobb of Chicago has arrived in the city and is registered at the Park hotel. Learning of his arrival a representative of the Tribune *called on him at his room. He was courteously received and when his purpose was made known the architect kindly unrolled the plans and gave the following description:*

The house is situated on Third street, between First and Second avenues north. It extends along Third street seventy feet and is 115 feet deep. Of the seventy feet on the street sixty compose the frontage and ten are devoted to an entrance leading to the dressing-rooms.

The auditorium proper is located on the ground floor and is reached by an entrance on Third street. This entrance is sixteen feet deep by twenty feet in width. On the left-hand side is a ticket office, furnished with a window, from which tickets to the lower auditorium and balcony are sold. From this same box-office, but from another window tickets to the gallery are sold. On the opposite side of the grand entrance the manager's office is situated. The auditorium is sixty by seventy feet, and the lower part is divided into a parquet and parquet circle. The seating capacity of this lower portion is 500. The balcony accommodates 375 and the gallery 500. The house will therefore seat 1,375 people.

The cutting off of ten feet of the front on the side next the alley has several advantages. It makes an excellent actors' exit and there being no rooms behind the stage gives an opportunity for perfect light and ventilation. Besides this it locates the dressing rooms very conveniently. Of these, four are on the ground floor, six are above the stage and three are placed in the basement, under the stage and will be reserved for minstrel purposes.

The stage is 70 feet long and 42 deep. This width, the architect says, gives ample opportunity to produce, without curtailing or diminishing scenic or spectacular effects, any attraction which can show at Helena, Butte or indeed at any leading point on the way across the continent. The height to the rigging loft is 50 feet and the space between will easily contain the longest and widest drops. The scenic grooves will be adjustable, double-jointed and will move from 16 to 26 feet in height, thus insuring an easy shifting of scenes.

In the auditorium at the right and left of the proscenium are the boxes, four in number, two on each side. A long loge box is also placed along the front or the balcony over the lower boxes. The orchestra will be of proportions sufficient to accommodate twenty pieces and a piano.

The grand entrance is paved with acoustic tile. Entering the auditorium from this to the right and left stairs are seen leading to the balcony. These are five feet wide and, being built out at an angle, leave an ample space below for ladies' and gentlemen's toilet rooms. The balcony proper is reached directly at the sides and leads from these stairways and is divided into a balcony and balcony circle. It is also furnished with a retiring foyer or lounging room sixteen feet wide by twenty long.

The gallery is centered from stairways leading up directly from the front corners of the building. It is seated with pew benches and is nicely ventilated. The lines of sight and acoustics are perfect.

The parquet, parquette circle and balcony are seated with the latest improved upholstered opera chairs, furnished with hat racks, foot rests, shawl racks, cane racks, etc. In the parquet the architect advocates putting in at least four rows of divans or double chairs. These are for the accommodation of people who desire a close acquaintance, or of people whose physical proportions are so pronounced as to make one chair uncomfortable. Should the committee approve, the entire parquet may be seated this way.

A particular feature of this particularly handsome house is the proscenium proper. This is built in sounding boards, which extend into the auditorium sixteen feet and then splay off at an angle of forty-five degrees. Proceeding at this angle the proscenium meets and intersects with the side walls, then taking on a circular form it goes from the floor to the ceiling where it meets a similar formation from the opposite side. It is modeled after the famous Chicago Auditorium and is the very perfection of acoustics.

The house is to be heated by steam. The boilers are placed under the farthest projection in a corner, at the rear of the basement. The undercurrent system is to be used. By this no radiators or coils are visible in the house, excepting such as are on the stage and in the grand entrance. The architect will advocate lighting the house entirely by incandescent lights, these being the best for showing off decorative and scenic effects. Their perfect safety from accidental fires, and their clear, pure light also strongly commend them.

In the lower house and boxes, the carpets will be a rich body Brussels. The balcony will have tapestry and the gallery Napier matting. A two-ply ingrain will be used for the dressing rooms. The upholstery will consist in the draping of all the arches about the stage as well as all the doors and windows on the lower floor. Curtains will be hung in all windows both before and behind the stage. The fresco and decorative work are intended to give to everything what might be termed an amusement effect. The grand entrance, proscenium front and underlines of the balcony are all done and treated in a general orange buff harmony, the style being a light tinted Romanesque. In the ornamentation, antique ivory will be largely used, relieved by gold, silver, and nickel bronze, all blending in harmony and accord with the architecture and finish of the auditorium.

Outside the study of the building is entirely of stone. The exterior walls will be finished in rustic effects with skewback arches over the windows. This front gives to the building both character and effect and makes the structure seem like a house of amusement. From the front a broad porch

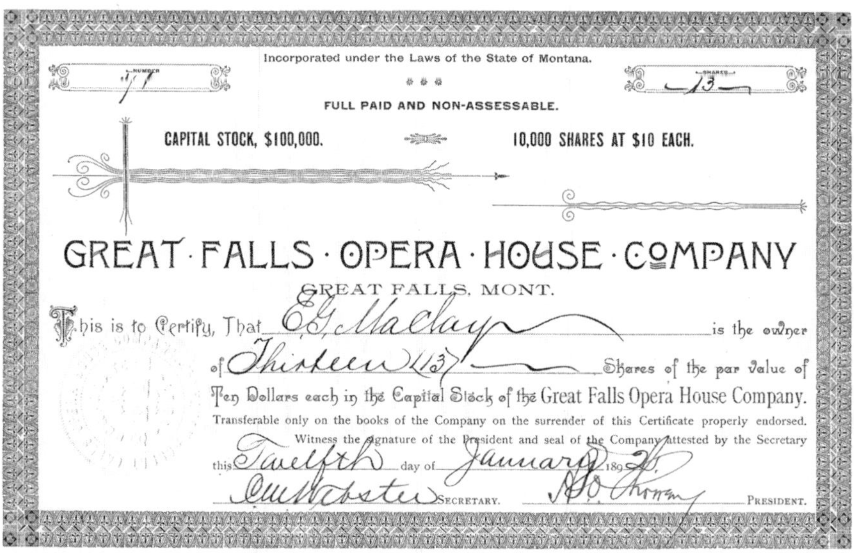
Incorporated under the Laws of the State of Montana.

Number 77 — Shares 13

FULL PAID AND NON-ASSESSABLE.

CAPITAL STOCK, $100,000. 10,000 SHARES AT $10 EACH.

GREAT · FALLS · OPERA · HOUSE · COMPANY

GREAT FALLS, MONT.

This is to Certify, That E.G. Maclay is the owner of Thirteen (13) Shares of the par value of Ten Dollars each in the Capital Stock of the Great Falls Opera House Company. Transferable only on the books of the Company on the surrender of this Certificate properly endorsed.

Witness the signature of the President and seal of the Company attested by the Secretary this Twelfth day of January 189

Secretary. President.

Great Falls Opera House Company stock certificate for thirteen shares owned by prominent businessman E.G. Maclay. *Author collection.*

projects over the sidewalk and furnishes at once an excellent location for a band and a protection from the rain for those below.

Outside stairs are to be built along the sides of the building. These lead from both balcony and gallery, are broad and roomy, and open directly into the alleys. They insure to the occupants of these places perfect safety, even if the stairs leading to the grand entrance should be blockaded by fire or panic.

The entire opera house is perfectly planned and doubtless the building will equal or exceed the plans. Architect Cobb will attend to letting all the contracts and will see the house fairly under way before leaving. Mr. Cobb is one of the best-known members of his profession. Over 200 opera houses testify to his ability. Among them are Heucks in Cincinnati, Faurots in Lima, Ohio, the Columbia in Chicago, the Grand in Minneapolis, and the Grand in St. Paul. Beyond a question the local house will also receive his careful consideration and will add another jewel to his architectural crown.[96]

CONSTRUCTION

The opera house company quickly approved Cobb's plans, and construction began. On July 1, the Great Falls Opera House Company was formally organized by Paris Gibson, T.E. Collins, E.G. Maclay, John Renner, A.E. Dickerman, H.O. Chowen, Ernest Crutcher, Ira Myers and W.P. Wren with a capital stock of $100,000. Architect Cobb operated from room 5 of the Bach Cory building. The contract was awarded to William Roberts; anticipated completion costs were not less than $50,000.[97]

By the end of July, excavation was complete, and sandstone was being cut at Sand Coulee quarry. Architect Cobb shuttled between Great Falls and Livingston, where he was supervising construction of another opera house. By September, the *Tribune* reported:

Scarce a citizen of Great Falls passes the temple soon to be dedicated to Thespis, who does not smile a large round smile as he pictures the scenes of beauty and delight that will soon be inaugurated within its walls.[98]

In mid-October, Peter Clausen of Minneapolis arrived in Great Falls to arrange the contract for painting the scenery and drop curtains and doing the fresco work in the new opera house.[99] Through November and early December, work continued in an accelerated fashion. The painted drop

The interior of the Grand Opera seated one thousand and featured this proscenium arch with scrollwork in stucco, six hundred lights illuminating the interior and excellent acoustics. *THM.*

curtain arrived from St. Paul on January 3. The *Leader* reported on opening night the next evening.

***The New Opera House* [Opens]**

It Is Complete in All Its Details—The Play Tonight

> *Notwithstanding the predictions of the creakers, the new opera house is completed in time for the opening performance tonight. The beautiful drop curtain was unrolled at a late hour last night and hung in place, the draperies have been put up and the scenery put in place and every detail finished, so that the house is in complete readiness to open its doors to the public.*
>
> The drop curtain is a work of art which will delight the audience. It represents a scene at Two Medicine lake, which will be familiar to many of the audience [author emphasis], *and when the two rows of incandescent lights which are set in the proscenium arch shed their soft light on it, it has a most charming and realistic effect. The carpets are down and the boxes all in order. These latter are not*

curtained in as usual, but are simply railed off, which leaves them quite open. This is said to be the latest style in opera boxes and gives a better view of the house and stage to the occupants, though somewhat at the expense of privacy. There are about 550 incandescent lights in the house, and several are lights that can be used in case of an accident to the former. The acoustic properties of the house leave nothing to be asked for.

The play tonight, "The Canuck," with which the new house will be opened, is well worthy of the house. It has met with tremendous success both in New York and San Francisco and will no doubt be a permanent favorite with the public.[100]

The *Tribune* raved in its review of the evening about the sold-out house and the "unprecedented affair in the history of Great Falls" attended by "the bone and sinew of the town."[101]

FROM RICHARD III TO THE WCTU

In the years that followed, the opera house, which quickly became known as the Grand Opera, hosted a wide range of events, from operas to theater plays, vaudeville, mass political rallies, boxing matches and the WCTU. While many drew large crowds and enthusiastic responses, an occasional gem rose to lofty heights, such as Mark Twain's lecture on July 29, 1895. The *Leader* reported:

Mark Twain in Great Falls

The readings last evening at the opera house by Mark Twain drew a crowded house and the event was the one of the season. His repertoire consisted of selections from some of his writings, told in the way that only Mark Twain can tell it. The subjects were: "About a Deceased Person," "The Jumping Frog," "The Grandfather's Old Ram," "Smallpox," "An Early Transgression," "Tom Sawyer's Crusade," "The Duel That Wasn't Fought," and "The Golden Arm." The utmost attention was given the speaker, and those who were familiar with his works keenly appreciated the vein of pathos and discriminating moral sentiment running through it all. Mr. Clemens, accompanied by his wife and daughter, and Maj. J.B. Pond and wife left this morning for Butte. The party will sail from Vancouver on the 16th inst., going to the Sandwich Islands and Australia where he

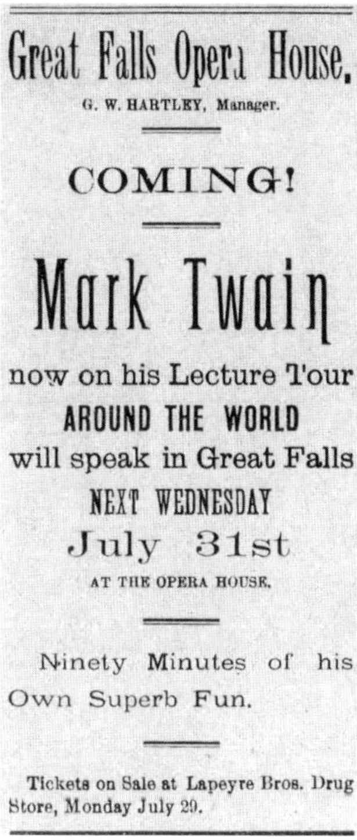

Mark Twain, on his lecture tour around the world, appeared at the Grand Opera in 1895. *From the* Leader, *July 31, 1895.*

has a nine month's engagement to fill in that continent, New Zealand, and South Africa, expecting to return home in about two years. His visit to the Giant springs yesterday caused him to suggest the building of a boulevard from the city to that point, lining the same with trees. This, his first visit to Great Falls, he expressed as being a most happy one.[102]

A "happy" visit or not, Twain was worn out and disgusted, as he later revealed to Martha Edgerton Rolfe Plassmann, the editor of the *Leader*:

An Ill-Mannered Community

Leader *Editorial. A Public Nuisance. A* Leader *representative in a recent interview with Mark Twain asked him if the continued lecturing followed by receptions was not very fatiguing to him. He replied that there was only one place where he "was beat," and there he was quite worn out. It was at Great Falls where this occurred and was due to the thoughtlessness—if we may not call it the discourtesy—of his audience. Long after the lecture was begun people came straggling into the opera house, to the intense annoyance of the lecturer and of all those who cared to hear what he had to say. Some of these late arrivals evidently attended for no other purpose than to attract attention. They spent their time in half audible conversation and only showed their good sense by leaving before the lecture was completed, thus giving those who cared to listen an opportunity to hear the finale. Mark Twain has often remarked upon the humility and meekness shown by the American citizens in the presence of a public nuisance; he has also urged that less submission should be shown and that the said American citizen should kick, and kick vigorously, until the nuisance is abated. Would it not be well for those of our citizens who are music lovers or who go to theater or lecture for any other reason than to be noticed to follow the advice of the humorist and enter a protest against the late comers or those who mistake such entertainments as we have*

The Grand Opera, fondly remembered for performances by Al Jolson, George M. Cohan, Mark Twain and many others, is featured in this model by artist Josef Dvorak. *Author photo.*

> *mentioned for* conversaciones*?…We can ill afford to have the reputation of being an ill-mannered community because some of our citizens do not know how to conduct themselves at public gatherings.*[103]

EVOLVING ENTERTAINMENT

As the decades passed, vaudeville and minstrel shows gave way to movies, and the Grand Opera changed with the times. Cold, drizzly rain forced

Memorial Day services into the Grand Opera on occasion. Young Stanley Ketchel won the hearts of local boxing fans with his powerful punch at the Grand before moving to California and national fame as a middleweight boxing champion.[104] Overflow crowds greeted Progressive Republicans like future Governor Joe Dixon and Congressman Charles N. Pray, and Montana and the nation's first female member of the U.S. House of Representatives, Jeannette Rankin.[105]

FADING TO DEMOLITION

Theaters of modern design and construction came to Great Falls, like the plush Liberty and the Pantages/Rainbow. In 1931, the new "million-dollar" Great Falls High School, with its spacious auditorium, opened. In 1940, the Civic Center opened at the western head of Central Avenue, providing not only a home for city government but also a large-capacity modern auditorium. The aging Grand Opera struggled to remain open, until finally, in June 1955, lacking a historic preservation culture, the Great Falls "wrecking ball" came calling, and the Grand Opera was demolished.[106]

Chapter 11

ELECTRIC CITY CLUB

Just one year after the Panic of 1893 and the hard times that followed led to the demise of the Rainbow Club in Great Falls, the economy rebounded enough to spark the birth of its successor, the Electric City Club. The *Tribune* announced its birth and previewed its opening on December 1, 1894:

The New Electric City Club

It Is Practically a Reorganization of the Old Rainbow Club—
List of Members
Description of the New Club Rooms—They Will Be Open on Dec. 1

When the hard times came along and banks were closing their doors and men who had been in the habit of spending money liberally began to cut down every unnecessary expense, the old Rainbow club which had once been a very prosperous institution, entered on rocky times and was finally obliged...to close its doors, much to the regret of many of the citizens. However, since prosperity has once more visited the city a number of gentlemen determined to again have a first-class club house. The result of several consultations and meetings among those interested was that a new club, to be known as the Electric City club, was organized and articles of incorporation have been signed and duly filed with the county clerk. The membership of the Electric City club is largely composed of the old members of the Rainbow club, and the following are its officers:

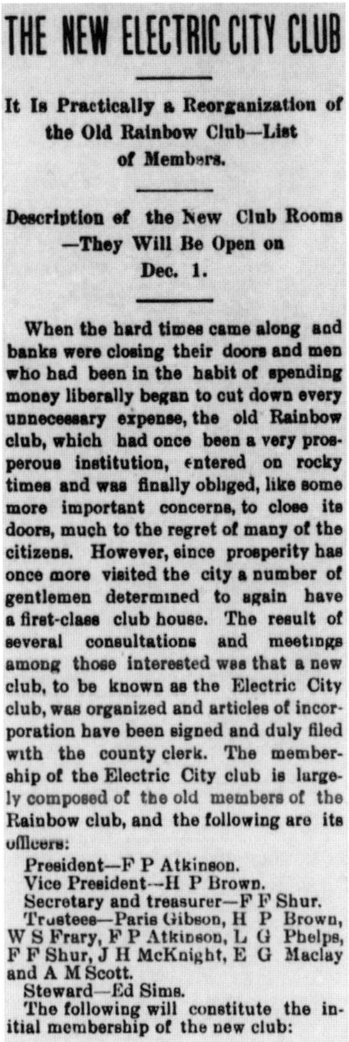

THE NEW ELECTRIC CITY CLUB

It Is Practically a Reorganization of the Old Rainbow Club—List of Members.

Description of the New Club Rooms —They Will Be Open on Dec. 1.

When the hard times came along and banks were closing their doors and men who had been in the habit of spending money liberally began to cut down every unnecessary expense, the old Rainbow club, which had once been a very prosperous institution, entered on rocky times and was finally obliged, like some more important concerns, to close its doors, much to the regret of many of the citizens. However, since prosperity has once more visited the city a number of gentlemen determined to again have a first-class club house. The result of several consultations and meetings among those interested was that a new club, to be known as the Electric City club, was organized and articles of incorporation have been signed and duly filed with the county clerk. The membership of the Electric City club is largely composed of the old members of the Rainbow club, and the following are its officers:

President—F P Atkinson.
Vice President—H P Brown.
Secretary and treasurer—F F Shur.
Trustees—Paris Gibson, H P Brown, W S Frary, F P Atkinson, L G Phelps, F F Shur, J H McKnight, E G Maclay and A M Scott.
Steward—Ed Sims.
The following will constitute the initial membership of the new club:

The Electric City Club for men opened in the Minot Block in 1894. Edward Simms was its steward. *From the* Weekly Tribune, *November 23, 1894.*

President—F.P. Atkinson.
Vice President—H.P. Brown.
Secretary and treasurer—F.F. Shur.
Trustees—Paris Gibson, H.P. Brown, W.S. Frary, F.P. Atkinson, L.G. Phelps, F.F. Shur, J.H. McKnight, E.G. Maclay, and A.M. Scott.
Steward—Ed Sims [Simms][107]

Club Quarters

The club have secured rooms over the Cascade bank [in the Minot Block] *and for the last few weeks the workmen have been busy getting them ready for the occupancy of the club, which hopes to be able to open up their new quarters by the first of the month with a banquet. A* Tribune *reporter was shown through the club rooms yesterday by Suprenant & Desilets, the contractors, who have had charge of the decoration of the interior. They have made a very handsome job of it and the club will have most convenient and elegant quarters.*

The parlor occupies the Central avenue frontage and is separated from the bar room by a partition of polished oak and stained glass, with ornamental panels and devices in wood representing electric rays. The room is frescoed in blue and gold, also in a design representing the electric flashes. The bar room is frescoes in terra cotta and gold, with rococo ornamentation. On the north of the bar room is a large billiard room, also finished in terra cotta and gold, with ray ornamentation. The windows in this room look out on the alley. The card room opens out of the billiard room and also receives its light from the rear windows. It is frescoed in buff, with gold ornamentation. The reading room occupies the west side of the building and contains an alcove for the secretary's desk. A lavatory is connected with it, and also a small room or closet for holding files of magazines and papers. It is one of the prettiest rooms in the whole suite, being delicately frescoed in pearl with gold and silver ornamentation.

Messrs. Suprenant & Desilets are certainly entitled to much credit for the chaste and beautiful manner in which they have decorated the club house quarters. It is not the intention of the club to do any cooking, but lunches can be ordered at neighboring restaurants and brought to the club house if desired. Altogether the Electric City club promises to "fill a long-felt want" and furnish a cozy and comfortable place for business men to meet, and also a place to entertain strangers who visit the city. A glance at the list of membership is sufficient to convince anyone that it starts out on a solid business basis and is likely to have a long and prosperous course before it.[108]

MARK TWAIN TONIGHT

Less than one year after the club's opening, a "stranger" graced its environs after giving a lecture at the Grand Opera House. Mark Twain, who was embarking on his world tour, spent an exhausting day touring the smelters, the falls, Giant Springs and other points of interest around the city, escorted by the Gibson brothers, and in company with his wife and daughter and Major and Mrs. Pond. The great humorist was pleased with Great Falls and stated that it was one of the prettiest towns in the West, resembling the Denver of a few years ago, except that the buildings in Great Falls were finer than those in Denver.[109]

AT THE ELECTRIC CITY CLUB

After Twain's lecture that evening, he and Major Pond were the guests of honor at a reception given by the Electric City Club. The *Leader* recorded the evening:

When the distinguished American humorist, Mark Twain, had finished his engagement at the opera house last evening he was invited to be the guest of the [Electric City] *club. There he held a reception, in*

Famed visitor Mark Twain toured Great Falls and was impressed by the Giant Springs during his visit in 1895. In the background is the silver smelter, Great Falls' first industry. *THM.*

conjunction with Maj. Pond, and a good many of Great Falls' citizens were introduced to him by Phil Gibson. All were pleased to meet Mr. Clemens and chat with him about late and early times, many who called having been old-timers like himself.

When he read in last evening's Leader *a reference to a hold-up which occurred to him while living in Virginia City, Nev., in the early '60s, he remarked that it was all a derned put-up job on him at the time and that he was opposed to that kind of treatment while in Virginia City, and he did not hesitate to tell the boys so then. Mr. H.H. Chandler of this city, who was at that time a resident of Virginia City, related this morning to a* Leader *representative further particulars of the affair. He said: "When Mark was held up, he was relieved of his watch and a small amount of change. He was ordered to sit down on a rock and not move for fifteen minutes. If he did, the top of his head would surely be blown off. When the highwaymen had gone some distance Mark hollowed to them: "Say, don't you think you'd better leave that watch so I can tell when the fifteen minutes are up?" The party did not stop, however, and two or three days after that Mr. Clemens left for San Francisco. At the stage station a large crowd gathered, surrounded him, and one of the number made a speech, expressing the regrets of the newspaper reporters and others at his departure, and because of his recent hold up and robbery, he was presented a watch, a small piece of tobacco, a jackknife and a purse containing two or three four-bit pieces. They proved to be the same that had been taken from him.*[110]

Beloved steward Ed Simms (*seated, foreground*) received financial backing from members of the Electric City Club when he opened his Electric Shoe Shining Parlor on Central Avenue. *Author collection.*

HONORING ED SIMMS

After more than a decade of sterling service as steward of the Electric City Club, in the summer of 1906, revered steward Ed Simms, whose eyesight was failing, retired. Over the years, he had gained the respect and confidence of and become friends with many of the club members, and with their financial support, he was able to open the Electric Shoe Shining Parlor in the rear of the Lapeyre Brothers' Drug Store.[111]

In 1908, the Electric City Club underwent remodeling and rearrangement of the rooms in its Minot Block home. The reading room was prominently positioned in front, looking out on Central Avenue. The billiard room was enlarged, while the bar was moved to the back of the club. The main entrance now opened onto the secretary's office and the reception room.[112]

ELECTRIC CITY CLUB CLOSES

On the night of March 31, 1919, the lights in the Electric City Club in the Minot Block were extinguished for the last time. The *Tribune* marked its passing with the headline:

Historic Old Club Will Close Doors

Electric City's Activities Stretch Back Over Quarter of Century and Are Closely Interwoven with History of Great Falls

Tomorrow will mark the passing of a historic institution in Great Falls for on the last day of the present month, the Electric City club will cease to exist after having been a factor in the city's social and civic life for a quarter of a century. During that period practically all the older business men of the city have, at one time or another, belonged to it and the extent to which it has been an influence in shaping the affairs of the community would be difficult to estimate. Men have met there to review the day's experiences and to lay plans for the next days, to entertain themselves and each other, and to benefit by the council of friends, but after tomorrow the habits of years will of necessity be broken.

The history of the Electric City club begins with its predecessor, the Rainbow club, out of whose membership the Electric City was principally organized in 1894. In the early nineties—a period otherwise referred to

> *now as the "palmy days"—the Rainbow figured more prominently in the city's daily events than it has in recent years. An old visitor's register contains the signature of Mark Twain and the names of other celebrities entertained by the club appear at frequent intervals among them being Louis James, the actor, Frederick Ward, and James J. Hill. These are exclusive of the long list of statesmen of national reputation and many governors, senators, congressmen, and prominent Montanans.*
>
> *In the early days the club was used for holding receptions and similar functions and there probably was a time when that feature of the city's life that could be referred to as social or civic centered at the home of the organization....*
>
> *Disbanding of the Electric City is largely due to the fact that but comparatively few of the newer residents of the city have been especially attracted to it, the membership gradually falling off during the past several years until the present roster contains only half as many members as when the club came into being 25 years ago. Lack of adequate quarters is considered to be an important reason for the waning membership. Different attempts have been made to obtain a home for the club more commensurate with its purpose, but the rooms over the Cascade bank have been the club's home during its entire existence....*
>
> *A meeting was held last night at the club rooms to wind up affairs and by tomorrow night the last proceedings looking to that end will have been completed.*[113]

Never a member because of his race, the longtime club steward lamented its passing:

> *It was a bad piece of news to me that the Electric City club was to go out of existence....The old guard who founded and for many years supported the club, were my friends and did me many favors. In the hour when my eyesight failed, they stuck to me and helped me by giving their patronage to my shine parlor, even though they had to go out of their way to do so. They were gentlemen in the truest sense of the word, and I shall never forget them and their kindness.*[114]

Chapter 12

BLACK EAGLE PARK

The first Black Eagle Park was a popular entertainment center located on the south bank of the Missouri River opposite Black Eagle Falls and operated by the Street Railway Company. This park, which opened in the 1890s, served as the site of early Cascade County fairs, horse races, baseball and football games and encampments by cavalry troops from Fort Assiniboine. In 1911, the city assumed management, enlarged and irrigated the park, planted nine thousand trees and added an improved baseball field. Although the name Black Eagle Park has since been lost to a smaller park across the Missouri River in the town of Black Eagle, its legacy lives on in Centene Baseball Park and the municipal golf course.

The *Tribune* featured the formal opening of Black Eagle Park at the northeastern end of the Streetcar Railway:

A New Pleasure Resort

The Black Eagle Park Will Be Formally Opened to the Public Today

Great Falls is to have a new pleasure resort at the Black Eagle falls. The grounds around the pavilion have been fixed up and transformed into a beautiful park, and certainly no lovelier spot could be selected for a park and summer garden. Nature has done about everything necessary to make it an ideal spot for visitors to spend an hour or two, and the little that was left for man to do to complete the attractiveness of the place has been accomplished with taste and thoroughness. In the first place a large tract of land has been

Top: Black Eagle Park was the early entertainment center of Great Falls, featuring concerts, fairs, horse races, baseball and football games, military encampments and more. *Author collection.*

Bottom: A collage of venues and events at Black Eagle Park. *Author collection.*

Opposite: An aerial perspective of Black Eagle Park (*foreground*) and the Boston & Montana Smelter (*background*) in a 1908 painting by an unknown artist, now on display at The History Museum. *Author photo.*

put down to blue grass lawn and a fountain built in the center of it, which will be filled with fish. A number of swings for the children have been erected and hammocks provided for the ladies. A large building provided with chairs has been erected for a dining hall for parties.

It is built on the edge of the bluff overlooking the rushing [Black Eagle] *falls of the river. Three large summer houses have been built 9 × 14 with lattice work and trailing vines planted to cover them. They are furnished with chairs and tables and electric lights inside. Seven smaller summer houses, similarly equipped, and vine covered, adorn other portions of the bluff and park. A man has been employed to keep everything in order and see that the place is kept respectable and attractive to ladies and families who desire to spend the afternoon or evening there. Every Tuesday and Friday evening and every Sunday afternoon, Robert Johnson will give an entertainment or concert at the pavilion. After the weekday entertainment there will be a dance and a small admission fee will be charged for seats in the main pavilion. The use of the garden and grounds are entirely free, and the public are cordially invited to make use of its privileges in any proper manner. Disorderly characters will be promptly barred from its privileges, however. It is the design to make the park a favorite place of resort for those*

> *desiring to have an outing and enjoy the beautiful surrounding and the scenery of the river.*
>
> *The grand opening takes place this afternoon and evening, when the Black Eagle band will give concerts from 2 to 6 p.m. and from 7:30 to 11:30 p.m. There will also be an entertainment at the pavilion by the Sullivan Lady orchestra, assisted by a company of specialty artists.*[115]

July Fourth that year featured a wide range of activities: the Black Eagle Band and Sullivan Lady Orchestra concerts during the afternoon and evening; an afternoon trolley parade at two o'clock; and a baseball game between the Great Falls and Belt "nines." The following afternoon brought another concert by the band, another baseball game and other sports, including running, jumping and foot, bicycle and wheelbarrow races.[116]

SKATING AT THE PARK

In the fall of 1898, a skating rink opened at the park: an area on the track in front of the grandstand, 50 by 350 feet, carefully flooded with ice about ten inches thick, in fine condition. Arc lights illuminated the rink, and heated waiting rooms for ladies and men were available. The grandstand sheltered the rink from the wind. A charge of ten cents was made at the gate, which included a ticket good for return on the streetcars. Skate rental was fifteen cents. Each day during the winter, the public was informed by banners on the streetcars whether there was skating.[117]

A sampling of some of the hundreds of activities at the park reveals many memorable games and events.

BASEBALL PARK

While a crude baseball park had been present for several years, it was in bad condition:

> *The field was covered with little elevations and shallow pits, and it was almost impossible for the players to know what direction a ball would take after once striking the ground.*

In June 1900, W.D. Dickinson, superintendent of the street railway, sent several of his men and teams to level the surface of the outfield and make other improvements.[118]

"PRETTY" JOE TINKER

The summer of 1900 proved memorable in Great Falls baseball history. That summer, the Great Falls Indians won the Montana State League, and they did it with a bunch of castoffs led by legendary manager "Honest John" McCloskey and a sparkling youngster named "Pretty" Tinker. Future Baseball Hall of Famer Joe Tinker, immortalized in the poem "Tinker to Evers to Chance," began his legendary career in Great Falls that exciting summer of 1900, playing baseball at Black Eagle Park.[119]

These are the saddest of possible words:
"Tinker to Evers to Chance."
Trio of bear cubs, and fleeter than birds,
Tinker and Evers and Chance.
Ruthlessly pricking our gonfalon bubble,
Making a Giant hit into a double --
Words that are heavy with nothing but trouble:
"Tinker to Evers to Chance."

Joe Tinker began his baseball career at Black Eagle Park, rising to fame with the Chicago Nationals as a key part of the legendary Baseball Hall of Fame trio "Tinkers to Evers to Chance." *Author collection.*

FORT SHAW INDIAN BOYS FOOTBALL

In the fall of 1900, football came to Black Eagle Park. The *Tribune* welcomed that first memorable match:

> *Next Saturday, for the first time the people of Great Falls will have an opportunity to see a football game such as is played by the colleges of the land....One of the games in which every advantage must be fought for and in which every play thrills and enthuses the spectators.*
>
> *The eleven of the Great Falls High School and the eleven of the Fort Shaw Indian School are to meet on the gridiron at Black Eagle park at 3 o'clock next Saturday afternoon, and an exciting contest is anticipated. The teams met last Saturday, when the Indians had an easy victory, but the High School team has been considerably strengthened since that time, having drawn on new and heavier material, and has profited by the experience of that game. The High School boys had never before played in a match, and were weak in defensive work, but their individual playing and offensive work was equal to that of the Indians. The average weight of the High School eleven, which was 140 pounds in that last game, has been brought up to that of the Indians, 150 pounds, and the boys are practicing steadily, under good coaches and expect to win Saturday's game.*
>
> *The boys believe that they will put up a game that will justify large attendance, and they hope to see a great crowd on the grounds, ready to cheer them on to victory. The High School color is the Yale blue.*[120]

The football game drew a rousing crowd of 325 to Black Eagle Park, waving their yellow, purple and red banners as the Fort Shaw Indian School triumphed over Great Falls High 21–0.[121] Black Eagle Park served as home field for the Fort Shaw Indian boys for several years, bringing memorable games against Helena, Butte and other high schools to the park.

FORT SHAW INDIAN GIRLS BASKETBALL CHAMPIONS

Great Falls also became the home court for Indian School girls' basketball during 1903–04. Games were played either outdoors at Black Eagle Park or indoors at Luther's Hall. Since Great Falls High School then had no basketball team, the Fort Shaw girls became the "home team" to many

Great Falls residents, drawing huge crowds to the games, as featured in the following *Tribune* account.

Undoubted Champions

Fort Shaw Indian Girls' Basketball Team Defeats Butte's Best by 21 to 5

Again, the Indian girls' basketball team of Fort Shaw proved their right to the championship of Montana by defeating the Butte basketball team by a score of 21 to 5, in a fiercely fought contest at Black Eagle Driving park. It was a fast game, strenuously played, but the bronze-skinned maidens clearly outclassed their pale-faced opponents from start to finish. The Smoky City girls had but few opportunities to throw goals and were not able to make good on those few opportunities in their throws from the field. The five points were scored on free throws given because of Fort Shaw fouling. If anything, the game was marred by repeated fouling on both sides in their eagerness to win.

Butte's best players were in the contest, and they acknowledged that they were fairly defeated….Minnie Burton carried off the honors of the evening for the Indians, especially by her accurate throwing for goals. Nettie Wirth and Belle Johnson also did some star playing. In fact, all of the Indian players are expert, and their teamwork is probably not surpassed by any other in the United States.

There is a probability of Superintendent [Fred] *Campbell of the Fort Shaw school taking them on a tour east next spring. Nothing definite has been planned, but an effort will be made to send them to St. Louis during the world's fair.*[122]

The Butte girls deserve great credit for the fight they put up, individually most of them are far and away above the average, but they have not team play down to a science and without that defeat is almost certain against an aggregation like that of the Indians.

Fully 700 spectators witnessed the contest. The line-up of the teams was as follows:

Fort Shaw		*Butte*
Genie Butch	*Right Guard*	*May O'Connor*
Belle Johnson	*Left Guard*	*Enid Waddell*
Nettie Worth	*Center*	*Stella O'Donnell*
Minnie Burton	*Right Forward*	*Frankie Dillon*
Emma Sansaver	*Left Forward*	*Tina Merkle*

Referee, C.W. Tenny. Umpires, C.W. Robinson, and Prof. Preston. Timekeeper, E.H. Cooney.[123]

MANY OTHER COLORFUL EVENTS

In July 1903, the Twenty-Fourth Infantry Regiment (Colored) soldiers from Fort Assinniboine contested a wild and wooly baseball game against "Cut Bank" Brown's Great Falls Maverick team before a crowd of seven hundred.[124]

One month later, Black Eagle Park became the memorable scene of an "Indian Sun Dance" and "Indian pony races" when the landless Chief Rocky Boy and his band of Chippewa performed there before leaving for the Blackfeet Reservation.[125]

THE MILITARY AT THE PARK

Four companies of the Twenty-Fourth Infantry Regiment (Colored) and six troops of the Third Cavalry, a total of about four hundred men, under the command of Lieutenant Colonel W.H. Beck, rode over the Fifteenth Street bridge into Great Falls on September 24, 1904, from Fort Assinniboine and went into camp adjacent to Black Eagle Park to join the Cascade County Fair. "Cowboy Artist" Charles M. Russell had joined the military at Fort Assinniboine and rode overland all the way in company with them. The soldiers pitched their snowy white tents adjacent to the park. Regular camp regulations were observed, and both the cavalry and the infantry performed daily drills, sham battles and other maneuvers in Black Eagle Park to the delight of large crowds.[126]

The *Tribune* covered the dramatic arrival:

> *The cavalry is in camp directly across the street car track on Eighth avenue from the Royal mills, with the officers' tents to the south, the head of the street being guarded by a mounted Gatling gun. West of the cavalry, the infantry is in camp.*
>
> *All was excitement and bustle yesterday afternoon, but everything worked with such precision that it was less than two hours after the camping ground had been reached before the tents had been set up and the little military city was fully organized. Hundreds of persons visited the camp during the afternoon to watch the work of setting tents and getting things in order, and sentries not yet having been put out, the visitors wandered at will.*[127]
>
> *Long before the call for "assembly," at 10 o'clock in the morning, the visitors commenced to arrive by streetcar, on foot and in carriages and*

A streetcar bound for Black Eagle Park picking up passengers on the 201 block of Central Avenue. The buildings behind the car are (*left to right*) the Minot Block and the Dunn Block, housing the Alcazar Theater. *Author collection.*

> *automobiles, and in a steady stream the camp was besieged until taps sounded, at 11 o'clock at night.*
>
> *The cavalry, of course, received the greater part of the admiration which was bestowed during the day, and the beautiful horses, which had been groomed by 7 o'clock, and which all day long munched lazily at their hay, as they stood tethered at a long rope between the rows of tents, came in for a big share of compliment. The quarters of the colored infantry were not forgotten, and the daily routine of work was watched with interest. The crowd which visited the camp did not thin out perceptibly until after 5:30 in the afternoon, when "assembly" was called, and the band played its patriotic airs.*[128]

In the days that followed, thousands visited the cavalry and infantry encampments and attended the daily performances, making this Cascade County Fair a memorable one. The daily race program featured the soldiers riding in rescue races, Roman races and hurdle races, followed by many other racing events, including for ladies and girls. After the races, at 5:10 p.m., parade was held at the soldiers' camp, ending the day's proceedings.[129]

GREAT FALLS' FIRST FLIGHT

On June 16, 1911, legendary aviator Eugene Ely, who the year before became the first person in history to fly an airplane off a U.S. Navy ship, came to Great Falls and performed a series of three flights from grounds adjoining Black Eagle Park—the first ever exhibition of flying in Great Falls. About five thousand crowded the park grandstand and vantage points outside the park to watch aviation history in Great Falls that day. The *Tribune* reported the action as Ely launched his Curtiss biplane:

> *Suddenly the word was passed around that the aeroplane was in the air. Instantly the expectant crowd turned with intense interest and saw off to the westward the airship sailing smoothly along. Mounting higher Ely swerved gracefully to the south, made a long circle, and passed directly over the ball diamond. A cheer went up from the throng, which watched Ely's every move. Three times the airship circled above the park. The last time it passed overhead the crowd could hear Ely shutting off the power. With a swift gradual downward swoop, the machine drifted toward the ground and landed at the place of ascent.*[130]

COUNTY FAIR MOVES

In 1906, the powerful Thomas Couch, who had brought the Boston & Montana Copper Company to Great Falls, promoted the development of a new fairground with a horse racing track on his land two miles northwest of Great Falls. The Cascade County Fair moved to this new location and remained there until the North Montana Fair moved to today's Expopark location in 1931.

CITY OWNERSHIP

The park board planted ten thousand trees in Black Eagle Park in 1911 when the City of Great Falls took over Black Eagle Park as part of its plan to complete Valeria Way as a cross-town driveway connecting the parks across the city. Over the years, many other facilities hosted the fair, horse racing, football and basketball games and aircraft demonstrations, replacing Black Eagle Park. By the spring of 1938, Black Eagle Park had evolved into a planned municipal golf course and the second location for American Legion Baseball Park, which was relocated from the nearby Montana Power Park at Eighth Avenue North and Twenty-Fifth Street. Great Falls Municipal Golf Couse and Centene Baseball Stadium continue at the site to this day; however, eventually, the park's name transferred across the Missouri River to the Black Eagle community.[131]

Chapter 13

LUTHER'S HALL

Opened as a dance hall, Luther's Hall gained fame as the "indoor homecourt" for the world champion Fort Shaw Indian School girls' basketball team. Martin Herman (M.H.) Luther came to Great Falls from Fargo, Dakota Territory, in the spring of 1888. He bought property on the corner of First Avenue South and Second Street and hired architect F.M. Morgan to design and Whitman G. "Vinegar" Jones to build a two-story brick-veneer block for three stores, to be competed in June.[132]

In Luther's first building, Luther opened the Five Taps Saloon, F. Krambeck operated a restaurant and J.F. Aaberg launched his Photograph Gallery. Luther's saloon advertised "handsome bar fixtures and all the appurtenances that go to make an elegant establishment."[133]

Luther soon turned his attention to construction of a second brick block at the corner of First Avenue South and Second Street across the street from his first venture.[134] Building on his previous successes, in February 1900, he unveiled plans for a third ambitious project, a "principal hall" for dances and public meetings. Luther acquired property at the southwest corner of First Avenue South and Fourth Street and hired nationally prominent architect Charles Emlen Bell to design and supervise construction. At the time, C.E. Bell and his partner John H. Kent were busy with the construction of the Montana State Capitol.[135]

LUTHER'S HALL

In mid-August 1906, Luther awarded a contract to Joseph Wagner for erection of a two-story building based on Bell's design, 50 × 150 feet with a basement, at a cost of $25,000. Luther's Hall was brick with stone trimmings, and Frank Coombs had the subcontract for the brickwork. Excavation for the building was soon underway. The first floor was divided into storerooms, while the second floor was designed for a large public hall, well lit, with a kitchen, anterooms, cloakrooms and lavatories.[136]

Work progressed through the winter, and the fine dance hall was described in the New Year's Day *Leader*:

> *The room is large and with a ceiling much higher than is ordinarily found in the halls of the city. It will have a floor built in a diamond shape, such as is found in all the well-appointed dance halls, and a hanging balcony will be constructed around three sides of the room from which the spectators may view the dancers without obstructing the floor.*
>
> *The room...* [is] *well-lighted and ventilated, and the accommodations for the comfort of guests are excellent. There are club rooms, dressing rooms, cloak rooms and smoking rooms, kitchen, and dining room, all conveniently located. Dumb waiters lead from the buffet to the anterooms.*[137]

The formal opening of Luther's Hall took place on February 12, 1901, with a grand ball given by the Black Eagle Band. More than two hundred people attended opening night, dancing into the early hours of the morning. The hall was beautifully decorated with bunting, palms and autumn leaves. The floor of the dance hall featured specially prepared hardwood.

The first floor housed the restaurant and buffet, both of which were opened during the ball. The fixtures were elegant, of solid oak and fine glassware. Luther stocked and made available fine wines, liquors and cigars.

The restaurant, managed by B. Feryan, served supper for the dance. Feryan specialized in catering for dances, banquets, weddings and other social events and serving meals at regular hours, as well as short orders.[138]

The night following the opening, Luther's Hall featured a masquerade ball by the Sons of Herman with a capacity crowd. The *Leader* reported:

> *Over 800 people passed through the doors and, though for a time the crush was great, the size of the hall was large enough to give room for every one present to take a chance. The costumes of the maskers*

Above: Luther's Hall, with its large hardwood dance floor, quickly became popular for a wide range of events, including two charity dances: a grand ball by the local labor council and a dance by the Grand Army of the Republic to raise funds for placing headstones on soldiers' graves. *From the* Tribune, *October 18, 1902.*

Left: A concert and ball heralded the opening of "Luther Hall" on February 12, 1901. *From the* Leader, *February 12, 1901.*

were varied—the clown, the friar, the devil...the Goddess of Liberty, the flower girl, the cowlady, the Red Cross nurse, and the gunnysack girl were all in evidence and feeling quite well, thank you! Music was furnished by the Black Eagle Band.[139]

FORT SHAW GIRLS HOME COURT

Within a year, Luther's Hall was hosting a wide variety of events, balls, concerts, political conventions, boxing and wrestling matches and even indoor baseball contests. In January 1903, the very new sport of basketball became a fixture. Dr. James Naismith's game was just eleven years old, and Luther's Hall became the home court for the most exciting basketball team in Montana: the Fort Shaw Indian School girls.

Luther's Hall became the "home court," drawing crowds of eight hundred, for the Fort Shaw Indian girls' basketball team. *From the* Tribune, *May 8, 1903.*

The Elks and many other fraternal, political and social groups held conventions at Luther's Hall, and the hall later became the Eagles Lodge. *Author collection.*

Superintendent Fred Campbell leveraged experience gained by Josephine Langley at Carlisle Indian School in Pennsylvania to introduce boys' and girls' basketball at his Fort Shaw Indian Industrial School thirty miles west of Great Falls. The new game resonated with the Native American children, and their teams, especially the girls' team, quickly rose to the top among Montana high schools, even playing and competing well against college teams in Missoula and Bozeman.[140]

Since the old military complex at Fort Shaw, home of Campbell's school, had only a crude, dirt-floor gymnasium—and to ease travel for visiting high school teams—Campbell arranged for outdoor games at Black Eagle Park and indoor games at Luther's Hall. Thus, Great Falls' Luther's Hall became the home court for the Fort Shaw girls. Many Great Falls residents "adopted" the Fort Shaw girls as "their" team, cheering on their dynamic brand of basketball, since Great Falls High School was slow to develop basketball teams.

FIRST BASKETBALL GAME

Most spectators in Montana had never watched a basketball game. A *Leader* sportswriter described the action in Luther's Hall during the first basketball game ever played in the Electric City:

> *Talk about excitement! Two wrestling matches, a football slaughter, three ping-pong tournaments, a ladies' whist contest, a pink tea, and one Schubert musical recital combined, would fall short in comparison with one game of basketball as it is played. It was the first game ever seen in Great Falls, but there will be others. Five hundred and forty people paid cash at the box office for admission last night, besides those who had purchased tickets previously, so that in all there were over seven hundred people present, and the hall was packed like a sardine box.…It was a success from a box office standpoint, and the shouting and enthusiasm would indicate that it also was a success from the audience point of view.…*
>
> *For real fun and a chance to howl naturally, without appearing a rude, untamed person from Greater New York, basketball is the unadulterated essence of the proper thing and its initial appearance in Great Falls created a furor.*[141]

A POPULAR HALL

For about fifteen years, Luther's Hall remained a popular dance hall and a busy event center for social events, fraternal meetings, sporting events and political rallies, like those of the newly popular Socialist Party. Nationally prominent politicians arrived in Great Falls and either appeared in the larger-capacity Grand Opera or, like Senator Robert M. LaFollette in October 1909, at Luther's Hall. In February 1911, Martin Luther retired, selling his saloon across the street at 12 Fourth Street South. In failing health, five years later, in July 1916, Luther passed away.[142]

At various times, the ground floor of Luther's Hall housed a butcher shop, theater, meat market, bowling alley, cigar store, grocery, hat shop, tea store and saddlery.

ODEON BALL ROOM

While Luther's Hall continued operations, in the aftermath of World War I and just before the Roaring Twenties dawned, it was rebranded the Odeon Ball Room and underwent major remodeling in a transformation

> *from a mere dance hall to a beautiful ball room at a cost of about \$15,000. The dance floor was the largest in Great Falls at 50 × 145 feet in dimension with built in seats around the side. The orchestra stand is in the center of the floor, so that the music can be heard equally well in any part of the hall. The newly formed Knights of Pleasure dance club took the lease on the Odeon.*[143]

GRANADA DANCE HALL AND EAGLES LODGE

More changes came in 1927 when the Odeon was remodeled once again and became the Granada Dance Hall.[144]

The Granada Dance Hall continued operations until September 1931. when it was leased by the Fraternal Order of Eagles No. 14 for use as their Lodge home.[145] In 1939, the Eagles purchased the property from Luther's family, and it remained Eagles Hall until 1965, when the Eagles constructed Eagles Manor to serve as an Eagles Lodge and retirement home. Eagles Hall was demolished in November 1965 to provide a parking lot as part of a city "park and shop" program and for bank customers.[146] The site served as a parking lot until 2000, when a 311-car parking garage was built on the site. In an urban archaeology project, Candi Zion sifted through buried treasures from the past at the site, finding memorabilia such as spittoons and whiskey bottles before construction of the parking garage.[147]

Chapter 14

SILVER DOLLAR SALOON AND BILL RANCE

The great social experiment that was national Prohibition led to one unintended consequence, a dramatic rise in organized crime, and one intended consequence, the demise of many of the West's most memorable saloons, including one of Charles M. Russell's favorite watering holes, the Silver Dollar in Great Falls. Both consequences were tragic.

END OF AN ERA, BIRTH OF A LEGEND

On January 1, 1919, no business was being conducted at the Silver Dollar Saloon. The door was locked. It was quiet as a tomb. Prohibition in Montana took effect that day, one year earlier than nationally, and the Silver Dollar Saloon was empty and out of business. The *Tribune* set the stage with this eulogy:

Licensed Liquor Dealers Get Ready to Obey Prohibition Edict on Dec. 31
W.H. (Silver Dollar) Rance

If there is a saloonist in northern Montana better known than William H. Rance he has been posted in the directory. They call him Bill Rance and he answers quickly by that title because he has heard it more frequently than

The Silver Dollar Saloon. *From the* Tribune, *October 24, 1982.*

anything else unless it were Rance. Bill Rance is almost as well known in the north country as he is in Montana. He lived for a considerable period in Winnipeg and has lived also at Lethbridge and Edmonton, but for nearly 30 years, Bill Rance has lived in Great Falls. For 25 years he has been in the licensed saloon business at 221 Central avenue in the Silver Dollar. For a long period, until the death of the senior member of the partnership, the Silver Dollar was owned by Philips & Rance, the senior member being Mandeville Philips, long in the saloon business in this state. After Mr. Philips' death at Santa Monica, California, a couple of years ago, Mr. Rance became the sole owner and has since conducted the Silver Dollar as his individual property.

Few saloons in the northwest have been visited by more distinguished people than has the Silver Dollar. This has been the result of the display there of the splendid array of art that Mr. Rance has collected, chief among the features being pieces from the brush, pen and modeling table of Charles M. Russell, the city's distinguished artist. Mr. Rance and Mr. Russell have long been close friends and in this friendship has been woven some most interesting pieces of art in the form of illustrated letters. When Mr. Russell travels, either back to the gay city of Gotham, or perchance crosses over to London town, he never forgets to write to his friend Rance and when he writes he embellishes his letters with some interesting little study in color, sometimes his inspirations of the travel on the boat, sometimes his picture of traffic in a busy thorofare and sometimes an amusing comparison of things as they are with things as they used to be. On receipt of one of those letters which already have become art treasures, Mr. Rance first reads and enjoys and then he hastens to an art studio and has the letter protected in a frame under glass. These are the pieces that have afforded many distinguished men a close view of the city's great artist and also an interesting angle of the Silver Dollar Saloon. There have been railroad presidents, statesmen, bankers, jurists, men of note in every line of professional or public endeavor as visitors to the Silver Dollar saloon to look over the art and perchance to look over the bar while they took a smile with the barkeep.

The Silver Dollar will be converted to new lines when the doors close on December 31, and Proprietor Rance will have some well smoothed silver dollars the distinguished mark of the entrance as lasting souvenirs of the fact that the Silver Dollar saloon lived up to its name for there were always silver dollars there.[148]

Bill Rance had begun the closing two days earlier by removing his great art collection, as covered by the *Tribune*:

Art Collection Makes a Change

Removal of the Valuable Pieces From Silver Dollar Leaves Odd Appearance

Perhaps no greater transformation will be wrought in the months to come than was wrought early yesterday morning in the Silver Dollar saloon. Those who betimes visited bar rooms—it is proper now to use the past tense—know that William H. Rance, proprietor of the Silver Dollar, owns one of the choicest collections of Russell's art that can be found. It has a personal angle that can be gotten only in such collection as owned by Mr. Rance, for most of it consists of letters of personal and intimate character to Rance from his longtime friend, the artist, and the art consists in the embellishment of the letters with the artist's personal views.

While Mr. Rance always conducted an orderly place, he and his friends knew there were possibilities of a rough crowd being abroad and that if such a thing happened there would also be possibilities of danger to the art collection which has been viewed by hundreds from every section of the country. Accordingly, he yesterday morning removed all the pieces to safety and the visitors to the Silver Dollar yesterday saw a changed place. It didn't look like the same. It, however, drew its usual crowd and Mr. Rance had sold all his stock before 8:30 last night, and at 9 the door was locked, and the Silver Dollar saloon passed into history. It didn't require any visit of the police to put it under the wire in compliance with the prohibition law.

"In the third of a century that I have been in the licensed liquor business, I have tried to conduct an orderly place," said Mr. Rance last night, "and we will just close the doors now and avoid any possibility of anyone thinking we infringed on the dry law. While I have been in the business, I have always tried to be fair with those employed by me and I believe the boys who have worked for me will tell you that I have treated them pretty well, always. I am going out of business in the strictest sense of the term. Just what I may do is not much matter just now. The law says I must quit the liquor business and I acquiesce in the rule of law. But when I quit tonight at 8:30, or about that time, I quit. I have no goods stored and so far as I am concerned, I am going to let the state go dry and be dry. About the only thing I have to do now is to mine silver—you know I have a few 'bones' left in the door at the entrance.

"As I quit the business, I take with me the memory of some of the best friends a man has ever found, for some of the gentlemen who have been patrons of the Silver Dollar are gentlemen of the royal blood. Whatever of the future, I shall ever keep the memory of all such friends fresh and green with good wishes for their success and happiness and as we pass into the new year, I hope that it will open with bright promises for their happiness and prosperity."[149]

REMOVING THE SILVER DOLLARS

Two months later, both the silver dollars and the priceless Charlie Russell artwork were gone. The Silver Dollar Saloon remained closed, never to convert to "new lines." The trademark Silver Dollar sign, hung in front of the saloon, was lowered and removed. One longtime resident watched and lamented,

The removal of that sign removes a landmark. I've known Bill Rance for many years, and I want to go on record as declaring him to be as "square a shooter" as it was ever my pleasure to meet.[150]

The elegant interior had been stripped of its rich mahogany and glass finishings, and the empty room retained only its memories as it prepared for its next occupants, the United Cigar Store and the Doswald Delicatessen Store.

CHARLIE AND BILL

William "Bill" H. Rance, owner of the Silver Dollar and friend and frequent host of Charlie Russell. *From the* Tribune, *December 8, 1918.*

From the day Phillips and Rance opened the Silver Dollar saloon on May 26, 1894, they took pride in the grandeur of its furnishings. As the years passed, the Silver Dollar achieved nationwide fame through Rance's growing collection of Charles M. Russell's paintings, models, sketches and illustrated letters. Biographer Dan R. Conway wrote of the warm friendship and shared interests of Bill Rance and Charlie Russell:

"Bill" Rance and "Charlie" Russell were old-time friends of early days in Great Falls. Before the artist became famous, he and Rance, who was the old-fashioned type of sporting man, were inseparable. Russell, while he had not taken a drink for many years, was almost a daily visitor at "the Dollar," and he never took a trip—whether it was to London or Paris, or merely to his summer home at Glacier park, without sending Bill Rance an illustrated letter. As these were received, Rance had them framed and hung them on the wall. These letters from Russell delighted many thousands of people in all walks of life for they contained the gems of wit and humor that made Russell almost as famous as a storyteller as he was an artist and sculptor.

Charlie's Letters

Dating back for years, they formed an interesting collection of the artist's observations on men and events as he traveled over the earth. There were letters written back before the days when the automobile was in common use, describing Russell's terror at being pursued by a horseless carriage in St. Louis, and setting forth his belief that they had horns to call an ambulance when they ran over a person. One of his letters describes life at a fashionable winter resort of Florida and imaginary adventures that the artist had with John D. Rockefeller. Another from London described graphically, his seasickness crossing the Atlantic, an imaginary conversation with the king, and the difference between London holdups and those in New York. He observed that the English waiters invariably said, "Thank you, sir," after receiving a tip—even a small one. "I don't know whether I am a 'sir,' or not" he said, "but I sure paid for it."[151]

Charles Marion Russell, on his Cow-Pony. In this photo by Charles E. Morris, the "Cowboy Artist" is mounted on his horse Monte in front of his log cabin studio in Great Falls. *Author collection.*

CHARLIE'S PAINTINGS

Besides the illustrated letters, the Silver Dollar collection contained about twenty of Russell's oil canvases and watercolors, depicting western life in the old days. Among them were these known paintings: *Scattering the Riders*, a famed roundup painting; *Teaching the Young Idea How to Shoot*, showing the interior of a Blackfeet lodge, with a young Piegan wife teaching her infant to shoot a miniature arrow at a toy warrior while his father and grandfather look proudly on; *A Buffalo Hunt*; *The Immigrants*; *The Round-up*; *Crow Horse Thieves*; and a watercolor of a North-West Mounted Policeman with a Cree family. The collection also included a four-part watercolor series Russell painted in 1898: *Just a Little Sunshine*, a cowboy and his horse resting in the sun; *Just a Little Rain*, a range rider herding cattle in a miserable rainstorm; *Just a Little Pleasure*, a drunken man having his boots removed by a woman of ill repute; and *Just a Little Pain*, a cowboy dancing in pain with a bottle of medicine used for social diseases in the foreground.[152]

In addition to the paintings, the collection contained many wonderful examples of Russell's ability as a sculptor.

Kid Russell & Monte, a 1986 statue by Buckeye Blake, stands just a short distance from the location of the Silver Dollar Saloon, one of Charlie Russell's favorite watering holes. *Author photo.*

A panoramic modern view of the Silver Dollar Saloon, the Alcazar and the Minot Block (later replaced by Davidson Plaza Park). *Author photo.*

THE FATE OF THE COLLECTION

After Rance removed his valuable collection of Russell paintings, sculptures and letters, he broke it up. William Grills of the Gerald Café, an old friend of Rance, received several paintings, and several items from the collection went to the Elks Lodge, where Rance was a longtime member.[153] The Elks received nineteen of Russell's illustrated letters and the book *Pen Sketches of Charles M. Russell*, inscribed by Charlie to Rance, with a sketch on the opposite page showing the two old friends arm in arm and a short poem.[154]

The dominant part of the Silver Dollar collection went to Sid Willis and his Mint collection of Russell art. Local historian Buck O'Connell believed that Rance used most of the collection as collateral to borrow money from Sid Willis and that despondency over not being able to redeem the collection led to Rance's suicide by poison on July 4, 1932.[155]

Chapter 15

MINT SALOON AND SID WILLIS

While national Prohibition brought the downfall of the Silver Dollar Saloon and its colorful owner, Bill Rance, Charles M. Russell's other favorite social hub in Great Falls, the Mint Saloon, and its resilient proprietor, Sidney "Sid" A. Willis, thrived during those difficult years and emerged to fame for its priceless collection of original Russell treasures.

At the dawn of Prohibition in Montana, the *Tribune* praised Willis:

> ***Sid Willis of the Mint***
>
> *Perhaps no man who has been engaged in the licensed liquor business in Great Falls has been more widely known than S.A. Willis, proprietor of the Mint saloon. Mr. Willis is known best among his friends and business acquaintances as "Sid" and throughout northern and eastern Montana those who have been in the state long enough to get acclimated have heard of Sid Willis and many of them have met him personally. He is a native of Kentucky but was reared in Arkansas and thru those two facts he explains his hospitable nature and his habit of making and holding friends. He has been in Montana for 30 years, coming to Miles City in 1888 and his first experience in the Treasure state was out on the plains where he breathed in the ozone as an employee of the Home Land and Cattle company and became a thorough Montanan. After about two years there he went to Glasgow late in 1889 and was employed for a time by A.J. McMillan in the saloon business.*

Above: The Mint Saloon, Charlie Russell's other favorite downtown watering hole, was famed for its illustrious proprietor, Sid Willis, and his collection of rare Russell paintings and memorabilia. *Great Falls/Cascade County Historic Preservation Office.*

Opposite, top: The Mint is on the left of this Golden Jubilee scene, with the offices of the *Tribune* next door and the sign for the Silver Dollar Saloon just showing across Central Avenue. *Author collection.*

Opposite, bottom: Mint Saloon proprietor Sid Willis built an impressive collection of Russell art, photographs, illustrated letters, models and memorabilia, selling many souvenirs, like this sketchbook. *Author collection.*

> *In 1894 Mr. Willis turned his attention to the political game as a candidate and was elected sheriff of Valley county serving in that office with credit to himself. In 1896 he had a complete demonstration that 13 is an unlucky number for in his race for re-election he was defeated by 13 votes.... That 13 votes caused him to leave Glasgow and come to Great Falls....*
>
> *When he arrived in Great Falls in 1897, Mr. Willis went to work for the Amalgamated Copper company, then operating the B.&M.* [Boston & Montana] *smelter and worked there until 1898 when he went to work for the late Dennis Dulin, who opened the saloon at the present site of the*

Mint and known as Dulin's. In 1902 Mr. Willis bought the Maverick at Second street and Central and after two years as proprietor of that place, he entered a partnership known as Willis & Burris in the purchase of the [Mint] *and has since been interested there as a proprietor, most of the time as the sole owner....*

Mr. Willis has arranged to remain in his present location and will, after from two weeks to 30 days' repair work, re-open, the place to be devoted to the cigar and soft drink business with a delicatessen store at the rear. It is Mr. Willis' plan to make this the finest place of its class between St. Paul and

Seattle, and he has already ordered the furniture and fixtures for the room. They will include a handsome soda fountain, elegant cigar stands and grill room fixtures which provides seats for the tables with partitions between them about to the shoulders of the patron when seated, thus making it possible for one standing at the front to always see thruout the room. The installation of this furniture will mean that the building will be newly decorated throughout, the front will be taken out and a great plate glass placed there, giving it a new appearance, and affording better light, and the rear, also, will be arranged so that the entire room will be flooded by natural light. The cigar fixtures will be placed at the front, with the soda fountain next and the remainder of the room given to the booths and tables and the delicatessen at the rear.

"I propose to make it a place attractive in appearance and one that will give the people service," said Mr. Willis. "It might just as well be stated here that when I say soft drinks, that is just what is meant and the place will be conducted absolutely in accordance with law; there will be no feature that the people cannot see and I propose, when the place is opened, to make it attractive to the man who works for pay and to make them feel that we appreciate their business. Some have talked about the soft drink business in places formerly operated as saloons as being only a means of dispensing liquor or conducting games. Let me say as forcefully as it is possible that when I open the new place there will be neither liquor nor gambling about it and furthermore, I will gladly assist the officers whose duty it is to enforce the prohibition law, in every way I can in driving the bootleggers and gamblers out, because we don't want them here. The law has said that I change; I am going to obey. Obeying the order myself, I promise the public now that no one is more anxious for others to obey than I am, and general enforcement will be my best asset in making the soft drink business profitable.[156]

CHARLIE'S TREASURES

Whether the Mint was a saloon or a soft drink parlor, its star attraction was a large and growing collection of the paintings, sketches, illustrated letters and models from the talented hand and mind of Charlie Russell. Large or small, Charlie's creations attracted an admiring crowd. Typical was the lifelike wax image the Cowboy Artist created of "Swipes," Great Falls' town dog, after his death. The *Leader* eulogized,

Left: Through his friendship with Charlie Russell, Sid Willis and his Mint Saloon gained fame. *THM.*

Right: Young Charles M. Russell arrived in Montana Territory in 1880 and learned cowboy life, earning a reputation as "Kid" Russell, the "Cowboy Artist." He married Nancy B. Mann in Cascade in 1896, and they moved to Great Falls the following year, where Charlie's artistic talent and Nancy's business acumen led to international fame. *Author collection.*

> *"Swipes," as he is known by, is one of the pioneers of Great Falls, and although only a common white bull dog, has more friends who will attend his funeral than the average politician....He is supposed to have arrived with Billy Bristol about 11 years ago* [1885], *and when he left "Swipes" became town property He never wanted a friend, and among the gambling fraternity he was a pet. When dog license time came around there was always someone to save "Swipes" from the pound.*[157]

Or the artistic treasure might be one of Charlie's illustrated letters:

> ***Russell and Rockefeller***
>
> *Cowboy Artist Hobnobs With Oil Magnate and Feeds on Crackers and Milk*
>
> *Sid Willis, one of the proprietors of the Mint saloon is in receipt of a characteristic letter from Charles M. Russell, the cowboy artist, now in*

New York. As the letter is illustrated with a very fine water color sketch, Mr. Willis has had it framed as a permanent keepsake.

The inimitable Russell this time is hobnobbing with John D. Rockefeller, the oil king, and he paints himself and Rockefeller enjoying a quiet cocktail together in a Broadway saloon. Russell has arrayed himself in a full-dress suit, although his familiar sash is much in evidence. The illustration is entitled "Me and Jack." On the door near the pair is a basket containing a bottle of milk and a box of crackers, the nourishment recently so popular with Rockefeller. The letter is as follows:

"New York, May 3, 1907.

"Friend Sid—For fear you will worry about me, I am dropping you a line. I intended leaving here several weeks ago, but I can't break away from Rockefeller and his bunch. Every time I try to make a getaway, he invites me up to have crackers and milk with him. He sure hates to see me leave. John sends his regards to the bunch and wants to be remembered to 'Piano Jim' and W.A. Clark.

"With best wishes to friends
C.M. RUSSELL."[158]

Dan R. Conway wrote of the Mint's growing collection of Russell art:

The "Mint" Collection

Some of the models and other pieces which adorned the old Silver Dollar have been obtained by Sid H. Willis, proprietor of the Mint Cigar store, who too, was one of Russell's closest friends from the earliest days of Great Falls. Willis has always been an ardent admirer of Charlie's work and throughout the years, he has piece by piece, acquired what is today, perhaps the most comprehensive display of the artist's work in the entire Northwest. He, too, has a score or more of the famous illustrated letters, mailed to him by Charlie, many models in wax and clay and numerous works in water color and oil.

Among the paintings on display in [the Mint] *are: "The Holdup," "The Buffalo Hunt," "A Desperate Stand," "Indian Women Moving," "The Price of His Hide," "Bring Home the Kill," "Hunting Buffalo," "The Watch on Fort Benton," "Rigors of the Roundup," "The Wild Bull Fight," and "Grouse Hunt."*[159]

THE "NEW" MINT

Ever the showman, Sid Willis opened his Prohibition-era Mint on March 8, 1919, with a ladies' night at

> *Montana's Finest Soft Drink Parlor, radically transformed as a place where women can bring their children for ice cream and soda and candy and be sure of service and proper attention.*
>
> *The interior of the building has been completely remodeled and redecorated. There is a mirror facing about the entire wall and a great mirror back of the soda fountain. There is a mezzanine at the south end of the room where Mr. Willis has established a curio collection with some pieces of art, mostly from the brush of Charles M. Russell of this city. There are firearms, knives used by hunters, Indian relics, rare coins, and other things of interest in the collection which is attractively displayed in a series of glass cases. This is reached by a stairway and is open to all visitors to the Mint.*
>
> *There are seven boxes with marble top tables where the ices and the drinks will be served but one sitting in the front box can see the rear and one at the rear can see the street, while those outside the building can do what Mr. Willis promised before the state went dry: "See everything in the room from the sidewalk."*
>
> *The remodeling has been done by Charles Moran, the contractor, and Mr. Willis says the contract has been very satisfactorily carried out. The painting and decorating have been done by Kaufman & Huba, and it is also well done....*
>
> *At the opening this evening there will be a six-piece orchestra to furnish the music and there will be favors for the ladies. The public will be invited to come and visit every department of The Mint and see one of the finest soft drink places in the west.*[160]

AN UNBELIEVABLE SIGHT TO YOUNG GEORGE MONTGOMERY

Gregoriy and Duna Letz, parents of future movie star and artist George Montgomery Letz, retired from their Conrad-area farm in 1927 to live in Black Eagle. Arriving the year after Charlie Russell died, eleven-year-old George was excited about this move to Charlie's town. His older brother Jim was a frequent patron of the Mint Saloon with its treasure trove of Russell art. Jim took George to the Mint and introduced him to Willis. George remembered, "The sight was unbelievable: showcases full of sculpture, small paintings, sketches, and memorabilia, and walls from floor to ceiling covered with paintings."

As the boys viewed this magical scene, Willis told them all about how he happened to acquire the pieces and details of Charlie's background.[161]

THE MINT SALOON

Prohibition ended, and the Mint celebrated the return to alcoholic libations. By the late 1940s, Great Falls was trying to come to grips with the powerful legacy of its famed Cowboy Artist. The Russell home and cabin had been saved with the help of Mrs. Nancy Russell, and the city debated an art museum dedicated to Russell's work. By 1948, Sid Willis had sold the Mint collection, which included about seventy-five pieces of Charlie Russell's work ranging from large oils to illustrated letters, pen-and-ink drawings, watercolors and wax models.[162]

Wills supported a new museum dedicated to Russell's work, insisting:

> *The place should be kept strictly as a Russell center. Anything else will ruin it because the tourists are interested in Russell. It is a disgrace for Montana and Great Falls to have let the Russell memorial slip as it has, and it will be a great mistake if the city does not do something to keep Russell's works here. A fireproof building should be built now because owners of Russell paintings cannot be expected to allow their paintings to be exhibited in the cabin.*[163]

LOSS OF THE MINT COLLECTION

The four years that followed were a nightmare for those who loved Charlie and his art. In 1948, the owners of the Mint and its priceless collection, George Sterling, Gertrude Egan and Maurice Egan of Billings and Gene Robertson of Helena, offered it to Great Falls residents.[164] When the money could not be raised, they extended the offer to the state. Led by Sid Willis, J.

Burke Clements of Helena and Dave Nettles of Butte, the nonprofit Charles M. Russell Memorial Committee Inc. was formed to keep the Mint and other Russell art in Montana.[165] Meanwhile, the collection's owners rejected out-of-state-offers and extended an offer for $125,000 to the new Russell Memorial Committee.[166]

In early 1949, the Mint Saloon was sold to Frank Kolar, a Stanford rancher and former owner of bars in Hughesville and Neihart. The collection was not included in this transaction.[167]

Moving forward at this time were plans for a Veterans and Pioneers Building, designed by architect A.V. McIver, in Helena as a new home for the Montana Historical Society. Included in these plans was a twenty-eight-by-fifty-two-foot room on the first floor to exhibit Russell's art.[168] The 1951 legislature appropriated $62,500 to buy the Mint collection if a like amount could be raised by public subscription.[169] Yet by the following spring, the Russell Memorial Committee had raised less than $13,000 and "threw in the towel, relinquishing any claim it had on the Mint collection." Ed Craney of Butte, acting secretary of the memorial committee, prophetically lamented, "It is our feeling that Montanans in the future will regret the loss of this fine Russell collection."[170]

Five months later, the Mint collection of Russell art was purchased by wealthy Texas oilman Amon Carter for $200,000. This would trigger the beginnings of one of our nation's greatest museums, the Amon Carter Museum of Western Art. Carter's interest in Russell and his art apparently stemmed from the 1930s, when the legendary humorist Will Rogers introduced Carter to Charlie's paintings. As his wealth increased over the years, Carter bought works by Russell and Frederic Remington, and when the Mint collection became available, he was ready to cap his collection.[171]

THE DEATH OF THE MINT SALOON

In the spring of 1967, the Mint Saloon was still operating under Jack Skelton. Though long without its prized Russell art collection, the Mint was still the legendary bar where Charles M. Russell spent many hours with Sid Willis and his friends and where the Cowboy Artist painted now and then in a room on the second floor. Yet in early April, urban renewal began demolishing the buildings in the 200 Block of Central Avenue. Buildings 212, 214, 216 and 218 Central were being leveled to the ground. On April 22, Skelton broke the news that the Mint Bar would close on May 25. The elaborate back bar and mirrors were donated to the City of Great Falls and survive today in the Charles M. Russell Museum in Great Falls. But the city had lost the great Mint collection and the bar where it all happened.[172]

Chapter 16

GIBSON PARK ZOOLOGICAL GARDEN

Great Falls began in the spring of 1884 as a planned city with a wealth of public parks from its beginning. The original plat of the townsite provided for a quarter section (160 acres) of land, extending for a mile along the Missouri River, perpetually set apart for park purposes. Riverside and Cascade Parks formed much of this original park reserve, owned and cared for by the Great Falls Townsite Company until they were deeded to the city on December 8, 1889. Riverside and Cascade were essentially one large park (later separated by a railroad bed) with communicating walkways, lying between the business district and the river and abutting the northside premier residential district. In and around these parks were driveways for horses and, later, automobiles, nearly five miles in length and maintained in splendid condition. Thousands of trees, hundreds of shrubs, flowering and foliage plants and numerous grasses and clovers were planted in these parks. Birds flourished in the foliage of the protected parkland: in 1906, some one hundred varieties of birds were counted in the parks.[173]

In 1903, the name was changed from Cascade to Gibson Park to honor founding father and park advocate Senator Paris Gibson. By 1906, the city's parkland had expanded to 480 acres, about one-third improved—still principally Gibson and Riverside Parks. The parks were under the control of a strong board of commissioners, appointed by the governor.

Early scene of Lake Gibson, home of many waterfowl, with a house on the island in Gibson Park. *Author collection.*

ESTABLISHING A ZOOLOGICAL GARDENS

In the late spring of 1906, Great Falls park commissioners began to form a small zoological garden in Gibson Park by purchasing eight young coyotes, which were housed in a small enclosure fenced with wire netting, north of the newly constructed ornamental lake completed that same spring. The plan was not to keep the coyotes but rather exchange them in a short time for four young wolves, which would be more interesting to the public.

The board knew that wild animals in captivity were fascinating and popular features in big city parks and determined to develop a small collection as rapidly as park revenues would permit. They knew it would not be practicable to secure exotic foreign animals, but they could acquire wild Montana native animals. They believed this small zoo would be of interest to both residents of the city, especially children, and visitors from around and beyond Montana, without requiring major investment for the animals' warmth and care in the winter. The board would judge public reaction during this inaugural summer before enlarging the selection with other wild animals in the next several years. The board believed "there is no reason why, in time, Great Falls should not have a zoological garden to be proud of."[174]

Among the fascinating animals in the Gibson Park Zoo were wolves. *Author collection.*

Within a month, wolf pups arrived at the little zoo, together with several swift foxes, inhabitants of north Montana's prairies. The tiny young swifts were about one-fifth the weight of a coyote, bearing black-tipped tails. They were kept in a small cage built close to the cage occupied by the young gray wolves, and a new fence was built surrounding both cages. The *Leader* reported:

> *The wolf pups seem to be thriving in their new environment and are now about one-third grown. Both the wolves and swifts are sources of attraction to hundreds of persons daily, a stroll through the park this season not being reckoned complete without a visit to the animals in the zoo.*[175]

Deer and antelope were added during that inaugural summer. At the same time, the park board began adding fish to the new lake. Trout and graylings were brought back from Craig along the Missouri River to be planted with fish from other sources. Swans, geese and ducks also populated the lake.[176]

Further expansion and improvements came to the zoo the following summer, 1907. The deer and antelope were moved to a larger two-acre plot with a game fence, seven feet high plus two barbed wires, making the total height eight feet. This enclosure or paddock was divided into two sections, one for the two deer and the other for the antelope, to accommodate the fighting proclivities of the antelope. Each enclosure included an acre, or about the space of four city lots, so that the animals had ample room to roam and graze. The house was separated by a partition to allow the deer to enter on one side and antelope on the other; a loft stored hay for winter feeding. A second antelope was added that summer.

Hundreds roamed through the parks, viewing the beautiful tulip beds in Margaret and Whittier Parks and strolling through Gibson Park, past hundreds of varieties of flowers, shrubbery and trees, around the beautiful artificial lake and on to visit the wolves, foxes, deer and antelope.[177]

The highlight of 1908 was the birth of twin antelope calves and twin black-tailed deer fawns, adding to the intense interest of visiting children as the little animals grew rapidly during the summer.[178] In the words of the *Leader*:

> *The young deer…have been source of wonderment and delight to many a childish mind, as well as an instructive object lesson in natural history.*[179]

Winter sports on Gibson Lake featured skating and ice hockey, often drawing large crowds: in the winter of 1909, a crowd of three hundred gathered to watch a hockey game. By 1911, swimming was allowed for boys and girls: bathing suits extending from the knees to the shoulders were required. Baseball, basketball, tennis courts, swings, merry-go-rounds and seesaws were all put in place in Gibson Park that year.[180]

The birth of six cygnets from one swan nest attracted national attention to Gibson Park. The Smithsonian Institution sent Ewen S. Cameron, a noted ornithologist and the husband of pioneer photographer Evelyn J. Cameron, to Great Falls to document the event. The *Tribune* reported:

> *It appears that nowhere in natural history has there been reported a case comparable to the Great Falls swan family. The great peculiarity comes in the fact that no other instance is of record where as many as six swans were hatched in one nest by one female swan and the brood thus becomes extraordinary. The Smithsonian naturalist made a very close study of the little feathered family and took many pictures. He also gathered all possible data as to the old members of the local swan family and will make it the material for a report which will be placed on record in the institution at Washington, and he will also provide several leading scientific journals with the story of Great Falls unique record of having the largest brood of swans ever hatched by one nest.*[181]

PART TWO **GREAT FALLS DAILY TRIBUNE** EDITORIAL SOCIETY AUTOMOBILES WOMEN'S

GREAT FALLS, MONTANA, SUNDAY MORNING, AUGUST 24, 1919.

Gibson Park Zoo Inmates Think This a Good World

No Troubles From Water or Feed Shortage on the Range of the City's Menagerie of Elk, Antelope and Deer

Swans Perfectly Contented With Their Feathered Costumes and the Pleasures Each Day Brings Them

Visions of a Hard Winter Have No Terrors for Domesticated Beasts Who Feed From Hands of Kiddies

Photo by F. E. Rogers.

Snap shots of the swan family and their summer home in Gibson Park and also of the deer, elk and antelope which inhabit the city's zoo and make glad the hearts of the scores of little children who daily visit the recreation center to feed and pet the birds and beasts. The island shown is devoted exclusively to the swans.

Extensive coverage of the Gibson Park Zoo in the *Great Falls Tribune*. *From the* Tribune, *August 24, 1919.*

"Copper King" W.A. Clark, himself an Elk, funded the presentation of two elk, a one-year-old male and a three-month-old female, from Butte's Columbia Gardens to join the Gibson Park Zoo in a specially prepared paddock.[182]

The park's population further increased, to the delight of child visitors, when twin blacktail fawns were born in Gibson Park on a June afternoon. According to the *Tribune*:

> *Three hours after their birth the little fawns were standing awkwardly upon wobbly legs, their big ears erect, staring at the admiring crowd. The doe licked them tenderly, polishing their little, black-tipped muzzles, and kept a jealous eye upon the people peering through the wire.*[183]

BILLY BUCK JOINS THE NEW YORK ZOO

Billy Buck, a blacktail deer born about 1914 in the Gibson Park Zoo, was shipped to New York in October 1920 to make his home in the New York Zoo. Billy departed Great Falls via an express train "in a nice comfy crate all padded inside, and with a bowl to drink water out of and a nice little manger to eat hay from." William T. Hornaday, the great naturalist in charge of the New York Zoo, met Billy and placed him in a fine little park with a wire fence around it and a nameplate on the gate marked "American Mule Deer." The *Leader* reported:

> *Billy Buck is a native of Great Falls, having been born in Gibson park five or six years ago, and his life has been spent behind the wire of the deer paddock with the rest of the deer folks. Billy has a magnificent set of horns, being six pointers, and looks every inch a blacktail buck....*
>
> *The New York zoo has not a buck mule deer within its confines, and Mr. Hornaday has been seeking one the country over, at last finding Billy Buck in Great Falls under care of Superintendent Henninhofer of the city parks. The shipment is in the nature of an exchange, and some other animal, bird, or plants will be shipped to Great Falls when desired.*
>
> *In Great Falls Billy Buck was known simply as a blacktail deer, but Mr. Hornaday labels him one of the "fast disappearing tribe of American mule deer," distinguished from the real blacktail through several differences, the ears being the principal one.*
>
> *In addition to Billy Buck, two of the swans will be shipped to New York this week, to take a place in the zoo, and some of the wild mallard ducks as well as the Muscovy, will be traded in for other varieties with the parks of other cities. Already the Great Falls swans are becoming famous, and specimens are located in Minneapolis, Portland, Chicago, and other parks of the country.*[184]

END OF THE GIBSON ZOO

By the early 1920s, the fate of the Gibson Zoo was being debated. Advocates for the zoo included businessmen, yet E.H. Cooney, the influential editor of the *Leader* and president of the city park board, proposed that the wild animals now kept in the Gibson Zoo be removed and the ground occupied by the zoo converted into a playground. Cooney argued that it was unjust to confine the animals in their relatively small spaces and that their chances for exercise and good health were impaired. He stated that a greater good would be realized by clearing the area for an athletic field and more playground equipment.[185]

Cooney laid out plans to establish a boys' playground in the space occupied by the animal paddocks and release the animals into their native wilds. The plan called for a baseball diamond, a cinder track, parallel bars, a trapeze and other athletic paraphernalia appropriate for boys.

The playground on the west side of the lake was proving highly successful for girls and smaller children—often, remarkably, occupied by over one thousand in the summer. Locating a playground for boys would give the girls' playground more room and would give the smaller children a much greater opportunity for enjoyment by removing the larger boys to their own field.

The Great Falls Woman's Club supported Cooney's plan, and this soon brought an end to the Gibson Park Zoo.[186]

PARK WATERFOWL CARRY ON

By the time the zoo closed, the swans, geese and ducks of Gibson Park Lake were a well-established tradition, and they have carried on until today. In the 1920s, the waterfowl had a house in which to winter, just as they do in today's Honker Hilton. The waterfowl house was in the yard of the park stables at the north end of the park, as reported by the *Leader*:

> *It was a quite comfortable affair, with a stove, high ceiling, a large water tank and a general mud decorative effect. When Gibson lake freezes up so hard that there is no more swimming all of the birds are taken down to winter quarters and live together in love and amity for several months.*
>
> *Jimmy Swan was hatched last year and spent the cold months in the winter quarters, enjoying himself very much and coming out in the spring weighing about 10 pounds more than when he went in.*[187]
>
> *While the Zoo at Gibson Park was never large, during its nearly two decades it afforded interesting entertainment and a lesson in natural history to all who cared to spend time watching the animals and swans, and it proved immensely popular with the children of the Great Falls.*[188]

Chapter 17

ALCAZAR THEATER

The evening of May 29, 1910, the Alcazar Theater opened its doors in the Dunn Block, featuring a five-piece orchestra to perform for the audience during the brief periods when reels were changed in the movie projection booth. *Thou Shalt Not Kill*, a drama; *Joseph Sold*, a biblical story; and *Mines of Mica*, a scenic subject, were followed by a comedy, *Stolen Fortune*, rounding out the silent movie fare that evening. Crowds packed the little movie house and its 419 seats, many with views flawed by load-bearing posts—just one of the many charms of the Alcazar.

Before the Alcazar opened in the Dunn Block, that building had already acquired quite a history as an early "city hall" for the new town of Great Falls and the home of Dreamland, one of the city's earliest movie theaters. Adding luster to the legend, the Alcazar became a legendary movie theater and a favorite haunt of Cowboy Artist Charles M. Russell after his visits to the nearby Silver Dollar saloon.[189]

THE DUNN BLOCK

Matt Dunn's new two-story block, constructed by William Roberts and Frank Coombs and located on the east side of the Minot Block at 205–207 Central Avenue, opened for business in late November 1888. Dr. R.P.R. Gordon, late of Edinburgh, Scotland; Sidney Carter Edgerton, a leading lawyer and son of Montana's first territorial governor; and others occupied the offices.

The night of December 3, 1888, the Great Falls City Council held its first meeting in a room in the rear of the Dunn Block, the new "city hall," with offices for aldermen, police magistrate Huy and city attorney John W. Stanton. Mayor Paris Gibson and Aldermen Fairfield, Beachley, Dickinson, Wegner, Matthews, Mitchell and Johnson were present at the first meeting of the city council there. City hall remained in the Dunn Block for the next year until the city government moved into a new city hall in December 1889.[190]

DREAMLAND THEATER

Various businesses such as Power & Trigg Furniture, Andrew Jensen Shoe Store and a bowling alley in the basement occupied the Dunn Block during its early years. In July 1908, the Dreamland Theater opened, presenting a popular film, a history of Irish patriot Shamus O'Brien. Soon, a three-piece orchestra became a fixture in the tiny theater.

OPENING THE ALCAZAR

The Dreamland went through two ownership changes before reopening on May 29, 1910, as the Alcazar Theater. With many innovations, promotions and rotation of films every two days, the Alcazar became an "institution" in downtown Great Falls.

On a typical night, a crowd packed the Alcazar and was highly pleased to see James J. Corbett demonstrate in moving pictures how boxing championships are won and lost. Two other films followed, with more entertainment, as reviewed in the *Tribune*:

> *Davy Jones' Parrot starts with a giggle and ends with a roar.…One of the best comedies ever portrayed in pantomime, the big western picture entitled "The New Boss of the Bar-X Ranch," holds the audience spell-bound, and the song which is especially dedicated to the B.P.O.E met with the greatest applause. The Alcazar orchestra rendered several classic and popular selections causing the guests of the cozy little theater to go away highly pleased with the hour's entertainment.*[191]

The Alcazar Theater in the Dunn Block, constructed in 1888, to the right of the corner of the Minot Block. *Author collection.*

DANCE LESSONS

In November 1913, the Alcazar introduced an innovation: dance lessons on the screen. The theater advertised its new bill:

> *Wallace McCutcheon and Joan Sawyer, sensations of the New York theater roof gardens and instructors to the "Four Hundred," will teach you The Tango, Turkey Trot and Hesitation Waltz.*
>
> *They charge $25 for a single lesson in any of these dances. All three dances will be taught you for the price of one admission to the Alcazar Theater.*
>
> *These dances are of interest to all on account of being so much talked about. Now you can judge for yourselves as to whether they are decorous or not when properly danced.*

The Alcazar's dancing lesson movies, in three reels, were shown in a continuous performance from 1:30 to 11 p.m., one day only.

The lessons followed a three-day bill that included a more varied fare. Pathe's news reel, "the most widely read periodical in the world," was the opener, followed by "Alkali Ike's Auto" a Western comedy starring Augustus Carney.[192]

MOVIE FAN COWBOY ARTIST

Adding to the Alcazar's legend is its association with Charles M. Russell. The Cowboy Artist had a long friendship with Billy Rance, who operated the Silver Dollar Saloon, just up the block from the Alcazar. According to local historian Buck O'Connell,

Russell perfected his skill at painting horses, people, and other animals by watching them in movies at the Alcazar, just down the block from the Silver Dollar.[193]

On the left of this scene, the Alcazar Theater sign is visible. *Author collection.*

NO PALACE

The *Tribune* captured the charm of the Alcazar when it nostalgically reported in 1963:

> *Theater patrons of today would do a double take if one of the Alcazar's programs of yesteryear were transplanted to a modern theater.*
>
> *They'd be more than a little surprised, too, if they were transplanted to the old Alcazar, which never was as glamorous as its name. It had no imposing marquee; it had seats for only 419 patrons and some of those seats were behind posts. Some chronic complainers thought there were too many posts, but the ceiling had to be held up some way.*
>
> *Some people also complained about the noise. Waller's bowling alley was in the basement. Many a tender scene on the screen was shattered by the*

Among the historic buildings demolished in 1982 by Blue Shield of Montana were (*from left*): Minot Block; Dunn Block with the Alcazar Theater, here remodeled for the American Legion; Marbie-Popoback café; Fischel cigar store; Hussman Billiards; Hotel Stevens; Grill's Gerald Café; Weise Hotel; and the Silver Dollar. *Author collection.*

crashing of the wooden pins. When a bowler rolled a strike, there usually was loud cheering, which didn't match the movie viewers' sentiments if at the time Rin-Tin-Tin was being choked by a burly badman.

Kids' Heaven

The patrons added to the noise. In the Twenties and Thirties, the Alcazar was kids' heaven. They booed the villain, cheered the hero, and roared in full voice at Laurel and Hardy, the Ritz Brothers and Wheeler and Woolsey.

Many of those kids of the Twenties and Thirties still have soft spots in their hearts for the old Alcazar, despite its noise, posts, and hard seats.

Another who remembers the theater fondly is Bob Bothwell, present manager of the Liberty Theatre, motel and restaurant operator and city alderman. Bothwell looks back on the Alcazar with a touch of nostalgia because it was the first theater he managed. He took over the job in 1938.

He remembers the posts, too. Because of them, the Alcazar had to have its projection machine shoot the picture onto the screen "on the bias." The diagonal angle of projection to avoid the posts distorted the picture somewhat, "but nobody seemed to mind," Bothwell says.

In its last years, the Alcazar suffered the ignominy of having its name changed to the Ritz. It was closed in January 1942, when the Dunn Block in which it was located was remodeled and the American Legion moved in. The Dunn Block was lost with the Minot and other buildings in that historic block in anticipation of a major new Blue Shield of Montana building, that never came to pass.[194]

Chapter 18

PANTAGES THEATER

When the Rocky Mountain Fire Insurance Building, owned by Set Free Ministries and known popularly as the Public Drug, suffered a devastating fire shortly after midnight on May 24, 2009, many were ready to write it off. It was just another old downtown building waiting for the well-exercised Great Falls "wrecking ball." Today, after several false starts toward restoration, the fate of the still structurally sound Rocky Mountain Building remains unclear.

Sure, the Rocky Mountain originally was associated with town founder Paris Gibson. Sure, it was an anchor building on the east side of downtown Central Avenue, designed by the city's premier architect, George H. Shanley. Sure, a splendid theater on the east end of the Rocky Mountain building, the Pantages Theater, had opened to acclaim in 1914 as the newest on the famed vaudeville circuit of Alexander Pantages.

ACHIEVING A DREAM

Many years ago, a little Greek boy dreamed of America as a land of flowing gold. Pericles Alexander Pantages left home alone in 1882 at age nine, made his way to a French port and worked his passage to Panama as a waiter on an ocean liner. France was busy attempting to dig the Panama Canal at that time, and young Alex turned his hand to everything to make a living.

He traveled up and down the South Atlantic coast, learning languages and adding to his store of knowledge. At age twelve, he arrived in San Francisco. When he saw the bright lights of Market Street, the brilliantly illuminated concert halls and amusement temples, he had no further doubts about his future. With musical talent and a love of acting, Alex determined to become rich and famous in the vaudeville game.

By the early 1900s, the boy was a man, and Alexander Pantages' dream was being realized as he assembled an impressive vaudeville theater circuit throughout the western United States and Canada. Pantages eventually became the biggest owner in the vaudeville game, with more than seventy theaters. He ran his vast business all alone, with no adviser, no consulting board: he was president, general manager, supervisor, inspector and booking agent all in one. He knew every act on his circuit: the number of people, their names, the props they carried and the amount they were paid.[195]

OPENING THE GREAT FALLS PANTAGES THEATER

By 1914, Alexander Pantages was ready to invade the young state of Montana. As a first step, on Monday, August 10, he opened the Pantages Theater in the new Rocky Mountain Fire Insurance Building at 605 Central Avenue in Great Falls. The date coincided with the city's golden jubilee celebration on the fiftieth anniversary of the formation of Montana Territory and the twenty-fifth anniversary of Montana's admission to statehood.

Headlines in the *Tribune* hailed the opening of the "most elaborate theater in Montana" as

> *the crowning achievement of the theatrical life of Alex Pantages. It is not only an improved replica of the Seattle and San Francisco Pantages theatres, but it marks the first step in the long-contemplated invasion of Montana territory.*[196]

The opening dedication of this, the newest and most beautiful of Montana's playhouses, occurred during the city's week of festivities, of bright lights, pageants and carnivals. Great Falls was not only the smallest city to boast a Pantages theater but also the only Montana city ever to have one. But the glorious Pantages Theater is long gone. Here is its remarkable story.[197]

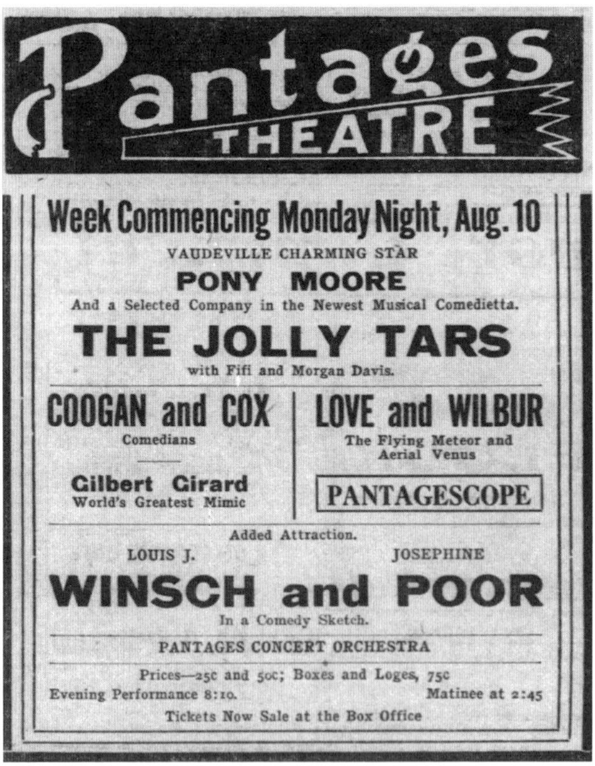

Pantages THEATRE

Week Commencing Monday Night, Aug. 10

VAUDEVILLE CHARMING STAR

PONY MOORE

And a Selected Company in the Newest Musical Comedietta.

THE JOLLY TARS

with Fifi and Morgan Davis.

COOGAN and COX
Comedians

Gilbert Girard
World's Greatest Mimic

LOVE and WILBUR
The Flying Meteor and Aerial Venus

PANTAGESCOPE

Added Attraction.

LOUIS J. JOSEPHINE

WINSCH and POOR

In a Comedy Sketch.

PANTAGES CONCERT ORCHESTRA

Prices—25c and 50c; Boxes and Loges, 75c

Evening Performance 8:10. Matinee at 2:45

Tickets Now Sale at the Box Office

Above: The Pantages Theater with its marquee sign, in the Rocky Mountain Fire Insurance Building, opened to acclaim in 1914, just at the end of the vaudeville days. *THM*.

Left: Vaudeville acts on the Pantages Theater's opening night in 1914. *From the* Tribune, *August 11, 1914*.

Opposite: Elaborate ceiling ornamentation in the Pantages Theater. *Gregory Photo. From the* Tribune, *August 2, 1914*.

PANTAGES THEATER

Built at a cost of $200,000 (some $6.2 million in today's dollars), the Pantages Theater was a creation of beauty, a model of elegance and comfort that filled a perceived demand for high-class entertainment at a reasonable cost, where leading vaudeville acts could appear for a few nights while en route to performances in the larger cities of the Northwest. Its opening strengthened the town's claim that Great Falls was the best show town of its size in the country.[198]

Construction began in October 1913 under the design of local architect George H. Shanley in consultation with B. Marcus Priteca of Seattle, Pantages' official architect. General contractor A.W. Miller Construction completed the "Pantages Greek style" exterior ten months later. The theater front was exceptional: terra cotta of ornamental design with a handsome marquee extending out over the sidewalk in front of the entrance and a massive, brilliant electric sign designed to catch the eye from afar.[199]

The main entrance opened on Central Avenue and led into the largest theater lobby in the city, twenty-six feet square with a fourteen-foot ceiling ornately embellished. "Flex-tile" of ornamental design covered the floor with marble borders all around, while on either side, a wide staircase led to the mezzanine gallery. Opening from the rear of the lobby were two wide doorways to the orchestra foyer, with staircases that led to elegantly appointed retiring rooms for women and a smoking room and lavatories for men.[200]

The interior of the Pantages was done in the French Renaissance style. Passing through the doors into the main auditorium, patrons viewed a

spacious interior with plaster ornaments. Renaissance art was displayed in the foliage as well as in the cornice work about the ceilings. The thirty-foot-wide proscenium opening to the stage displayed artistically designed plaster ornamentation on either side in bold relief. The theater, including two balconies, loges and boxes, seated 1,200, and every seat provided a clear view of the stage.[201]

The opening night gala on August 10, 1914, featured the best of vaudeville with singing, dancing and comedy, climaxed by Pony Moore's musical extravaganza the Jolly Tars.[202]

The *Leader* headlined its warm review:

> ***New Pantages Swings Open***
> ***Magnificent Vaudeville Theater Just Erected in Great Falls Starts Upon Its Career***
>
> *Great Falls' magnificent new Pantages theater at Central avenue and Sixth Street, the first Pantages house to be opened in Montana, made its initial bow last evening and those who attended the opening of this beautiful new temple of vaudeville saw new delights in store for the local theater-going public.*
>
> *With the new house apparently complete in every detail, the house orchestra under the leadership of Meyer Burnett furnishing delightful music, and a vaudeville program for the first night of excellence throughout, the opening was a pronounced success.*
>
> *There was no haste in starting the evening's program, so the members of the audience had ample opportunity to inspect the house and expressions of delight were heard on all sides at the admirable arrangement of the theater, its handsome row of boxes, its beautiful indirect lighting system, ample stable, handsome curtains, and many other details that combine to make Great Falls' new Pantages one of the most luxurious theaters in the west.*
>
> *Governor Stewart was to have spoken at the opening exercises but was prevented from being present by sickness. These exercises were brief.... Then opened the regular vaudeville entertainment program.*
>
> *If the standard of succeeding programs at the Pantages may be judged by the opening one then there seems little doubt that the house will be liberally patronized, for the first bill is a very strong one. The program opened with the "Pantagescope," presenting world's events in pictures that stand out marvelously bright and clear. Next came Love and Wilber, "the flying meteor and aerial Venus." This proved to be one of the best aerial acts ever seen here.*

P is for Pantages on the theater's decorative exterior. *Author photo.*

Gilbert Girard, "the human harp," is a wonder at manipulating his vocal cords. He simulates the chirp of the nightingale, the baying of the dog, the hoot of the owl and the roar of the lion with apparent ease. There is no noise that he cannot imitate and imitate well, and his act is a very entertaining one.

Louis J. Winsch and Josephine Poore presented a delightful little skit entitled "Not Trespassing," in which they introduce some clever dialogue and singing.

Coogan and Cox were next. They are down on the program as comedians and real comedians they are—not the alleged variety. It is worthwhile to attend Pantages' first bill just to see this clever pair. They have a lot of good dialogue, sing well and their dancing is great.

The bill closes with Pony Moore's musical scenic extravaganza "The Jolly Tars," in which a bevy of pretty and shapely girls is introduced.

There is a big company in this act that introduces a lot of good singing, dancing, and comedy.

Don't fail to see the Pantages opening bill.[203]

PANTAGES BECOMES THE PALACE FILM THEATER

Unfortunately for the Pantages, the crowning achievement quickly became a white elephant; vaudeville was dying as theatergoers turned to motion pictures. Disaster struck the Pantages less than a year later, when in May 1915, a sheriff's sale was held to recover possession of the theater and property, such as carpets and draperies. One month later, the Pantages was reborn as the Palace Theater, showing "high class motion pictures."[204]

THE PLUSH RAINBOW THEATER OPENS

About a decade later, the Palace became the Rainbow Film Theater, which opened on Saturday, March 13, 1926, with the film *Skyrocket*, starring Peggy Hopkins Joyce, under the management of Walter E. White. The Rainbow featured a "sparkling, fresh interior from ceiling to floor," a new movie screen and new projection equipment. The popular Rainbow Theater, with its plush interior environment, competed with the Liberty Theatre for decades. By the late 1950s, its age and lack of upkeep had begun to show. Plaster fell from the overhanging balcony, leading to injuries and a lawsuit. Owner Fox Montana Theater Corporation decided to modernize the Liberty, so the Rainbow's days were numbered. The Rainbow Theater, once the mighty Pantages, operated until 1964, when it succumbed to a combination of television and its owners' decision to replace it with a large modern movie theater in the new Holiday Village Shopping Center.[205]

DEMOLITION OF THE RAINBOW THEATER

The end came for the Pantages/Rainbow Theater in January 1966, when it was demolished for conversion into ramp parking for fifty autos inside the

Rocky Mountain Building. The first part of the demolition work removed everything in the building: the balcony, the stairs, the stage and the auditorium floor, up to the exterior walls. All that remained of the once mighty theater was the Central Avenue exterior wall with its eclectic Beaux Arts style of ornamental terra cotta, including the letter *P* for Pantages, leaving a striking legacy for the great Alexander Pantages and his famed circuit of Pantages vaudeville theaters.[206]

Chapter 19

TENTH ALLEY SOUTH

Prostitution in Great Falls was centered, early on, on the lower Southside, run by several influential madams in places like Rosebud Alley and Fourth Alley South. After the arrival of the Milwaukee Railroad in 1913, this area transformed into railroad warehouses. In exchange, the madams were provided with new brick buildings located on Tenth Alley South between Second and Third Streets. In this notorious red-light "restricted district" nine houses operated, such as the Harem of proprietress Hermine Vortman and the Klondike, under Annie Wolf.

BRINGING ORDER TO PROSTITUTION

A three-page handwritten document by John Stevenson Sr. titled "Tenth Alley South" sets the scene.

> *It was probably* [1912] *when Great Falls became aware that The Milwaukee Railroad as a part of its westward expansion planned to build a branch line from Harlowton, on its main line, north and west through the Judith Basin and around the north end of the Highwood Mountains to Great Falls.…Great Falls would be the headquarters for this branch line, with a "roundhouse" and an impressive passenger depot. This meant much new business for Great Falls and likewise an influx of labor during the construction period.*

Prostitution in Great Falls centered early on the lower Southside, under several influential madams, in places like Rosebud Alley. With the arrival of the Milwaukee Railroad, that area was transformed into railroad warehouses. In exchange, in 1913, the madams were provided with brick buildings located on Tenth Alley South and Second Street. *Cascade County Commission.*

Prostitution was then firmly established in Great Falls under the control of several very influential "madams." However, prostitutes did, on occasion openly solicit on the streets of downtown Great Falls, and their presence there was an affront to the good ladies of the town.

The coming invasion of the town by great numbers of construction workers seeking drink and female companionship inevitably meant a like invasion of females ready, willing, and eager to provide the companionship at a price.

Obviously, something must be done to control this situation, and make downtown Great Falls a place where a "decent" woman could safely walk. My father, Sam Stephenson, was the local attorney representing the Milwaukee Railroad. His partner, Ranson Cooper, was the attorney for Great Falls Townsite Company, which owned and controlled the unsold portions of the land constituting the Townsite of Great Falls and its additions. O.S. Warden was the owner and publisher of the Great Falls Tribune *(and its evening affiliate, the* Great Falls Leader*), the most influential newspaper in the state. An arrangement was made by and between these men and the madams (obviously verbal and not reduced to writing since each one's word was good) as follows:*

The townsite company would provide the land, and it and the railroad would provide the funds to construct a brick building at Second Street and Tenth Alley South to suitably house the Madams and all of their prostitutes. The madams, in turn, would see that prostitution was confined to this location, and that on the street solicitation stopped.

I believe the necessary paper work for donation of said land and construction of said building was completed when Sam Stephenson and O.S. Warden made a formal call on Ranson Cooper, at his law office, and confirmed the agreement as above set forth.

And the plan worked. The building, commonly known as "Tenth Alley South" was constructed. The madams and their girls moved in and opened for business. Open street solicitations stopped. The good ladies of the town were satisfied, and everybody was happy, because it all worked.

My father Sam Stephenson had a somewhat perverse sense of humor. In later years at public affairs where both he and O.S. Warden were present, he would hail O.S. Warden, loudly as follows: "Hey Doc Remember when you and I served on the whorehouse committee?" Mr. Warden was not amused.

April 21, 1987—John Stephenson, Sr.[207]

THE MADAMS AND THEIR BRICK PALACES

Tenth Alley South was selected because the Townsite Company owned land there, it was at the edge of the city's southern limits and it was just beyond the Milwaukee Railroad planned area. By February 1913, the first of the cribs had been cleared out of Rosebud Alley. Meanwhile, city building permits began to appear in the newspapers for the promised replacement brick buildings. Over the next year, the block known as Tenth Alley South was completed. The City installed concrete sidewalks and curbs on both sides of Lots in the 504 Block, as well as sewer lines. By mid-1914, ten houses of prostitution were operated in Tenth Alley South, listed by street address. On the south side of Tenth Alley:

104: The New Panama. Built for Louise C. Lloyd, and opened June 20, 1914, two-story brick rooming house at 104 Tenth Alley South, cost $9,800. Madam Elsie Mills, also known as Nellie Lee, managed the operation.[208]

108: THE KLONDIKE. Annie Wolf, madam of this African American "colored resort," had a two-story brick dwelling constructed at a cost of $8,000. The next spring, an addition was constructed for $4,500.[209] While the bawdy houses in Tenth Alley South normally operated peacefully, on occasion, there were incidents. In February 1915, a "house-cleaning party and drunken brawl" broke out at the Klondike. Five men were arrested and brought before police court. Each defendant disclaimed participation in the roughhousing, but Madam Wolf testified that one had broken several glasses by kicking a tray from the waiter's hand and another had smashed a fourteen-dollar piano stool by knocking it over and jumping on it. Two men, Oscar Peters and A.R. Sellar, were found guilty and fined ten dollars each, while the remaining trio was discharged.[210]

124: BRYANT HOUSE. Madam Sylvia Bryant had a forty-by-sixty-five-foot two-story brick building constructed at a cost of $10,000.[211]

126: THE ETHEL WARREN HOUSE. Ethel Condon, also known as Warren, the madam, owned and managed this two-story brick building, constructed by J.O. Ness for $15,000. Occasional insight into the lives of the young ladies, called "inmates," who worked in Tenth Alley South's "resorts" came from newspaper reporting. In May 1914, Margaret Ayres, an inmate of the Warren house, was initially thought to have tried to end her life by taking poison. An examining doctor concluded the cause was an "oversupply of whiskey."[212]

Warren's resort was locked up during a general closure of the restricted district in 1917. In early June 1917, Warren was arrested in her home together with an unnamed man. The booking sergeant entered her name as Ethel Brown as a courtesy to her.[213]

During December 1917, a scarlet fever epidemic swept through Great Falls. In response, city health officer R.E. McCarten arrange to rent the Warren building as a detention hospital. The hospital had ten well-ventilated rooms with a medicine chest in each, a large kitchen, a dining room, two reception rooms and a large dance hall—usable as a ward, if necessary. Hot and cold water was available throughout the house, which was fireproof and boasted beautiful interior finishing, partly furnished with oak furniture.[214]

In 1919, the Warren House was again opened as a joint city and county detention hospital for treatment of patients suffering from scarlet fever and diphtheria.[215]

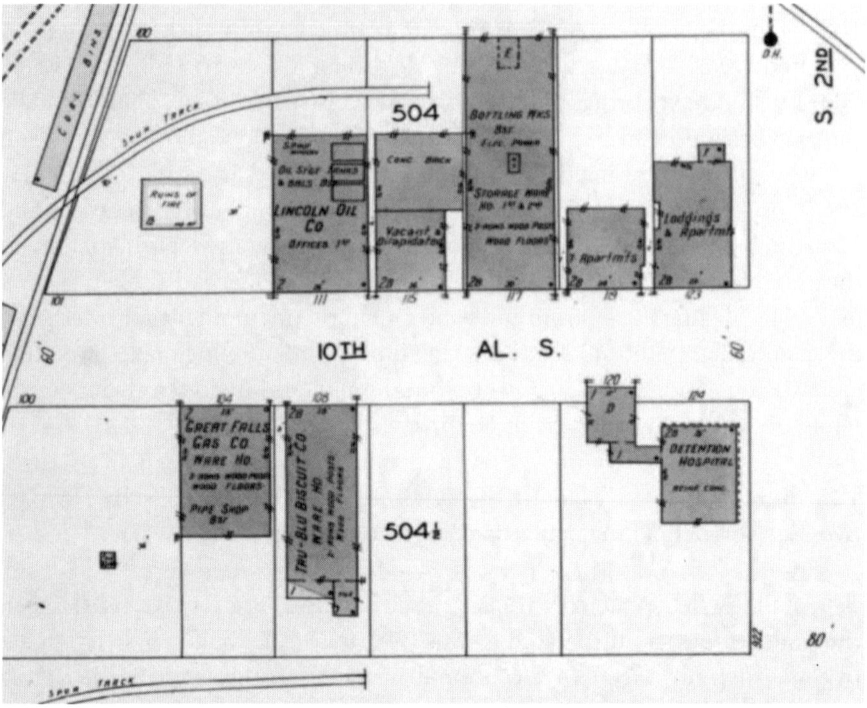

Tenth Alley South, shown on the Sanborn map of Block 504. *Public domain.*

On the north side of Tenth Alley South:

111: The Paradise. Madam Lillian Hunter had a two-story brick lodging house constructed at a cost of $11,200.[216] In May 1914, Dollie Nichols, an inmate of the Paradise, attempted to kill herself by taking poison. She was carried to the Deaconess Hospital in a bad way and recovered after several days of treatment.[217]

113: Rooming House. Daisy Smith, also known as Hill, had a forty-by-forty-five-foot two-story brick building constructed at a cost of $5,000 for use as a rooming house.[218]

115: The Midway. Madam Daisy Smith also had this two-story brick building constructed at a cost of $6,000.[219]

117: The Harem. Madam Hermine Vortman, also known as Lou Ashley, popularly known as "Big Lou," had a large two-story brick building, 46 ×130 feet, constructed, costing S22,700. The following spring, alterations were made in the basement at a cost of $2,800. Thirty young women were operating at the Harem when it closed in 1917.[220]

121: HAZZARD HOUSE. Louise Rockwell had this two-story brick building constructed, costing $8,000. Madam Dorothy Hazzard operated this resort.[221]

123: BRYANT HOUSE. Madam Sylvia Bryant had a two-story brick building constructed by Lange Engineering & Construction Co.[222] In 1919, this building was rented as a county detention hospital for smallpox victims.[223]

125: WARREN HOUSE. Madam Ethel Warren, also known as Ethel Condon, had this additional thirty-by-forty-one-foot two-story brick building constructed by contractor J.O. Ness at a cost of $15,000.[224] During the Spanish flu epidemic, beginning in 1917, the Warren House was rented for $100 a month as a detention hospital.[225]

RENEGADE GIRLS

By early 1917, some adventurous girls had begun leaving Tenth Alley South to operate downtown. In an early morning police raid led by Sergeant A.J. Trodick, Dollie Nichols, Maud Jones, Margaret Hill and Annie Gulit were arrested. The girls bragged that they did not have to remain on Tenth Alley South and pay a monthly fine when they could earn more downtown. Sergeant Trodick countered, saying, "We are watching everyone from now on and as fast as they leave the alley they will be sent back."[226]

RED LIGHTS ARE DIMMED

On January 8, 1917, Cascade County and city police officers raided Tenth Alley South to close it down permanently, acting under orders from Montana's attorney general, Sam C. Ford. The *Leader* reported on this shocking development:

Restricted District Now Thing of the Past. Red Light Closed On Orders of Sheriff

The Great Falls restricted district, Tenth alley south, was closed at 11:30 a.m. today on order of Sheriff Kommers and Chief of Police Pontet, acting under instructions from Attorney General S.C. Ford, who has ordered that [the new Lewis abatement] *law be enforced.*

The order of Sheriff Kommers is a definite one, and the inmates are instructed that should the houses be opened hereafter at any time all persons found there will be arrested and taken to the county jail together with all available evidence, for prosecution under the law, the owners of the house where the arrest is made being specifically held for punishment under the law.

Following the coming of the Milwaukee railroad to Great Falls, and the purchase of the restricted district for warehouse and yardage purposes, costly brick houses were erected on Tenth alley south, and that section was given over to that class, under police surveillance; the houses now number about 10 and are said to be valued at about $200,000.

According to the 1916 annual police report…there were about 138 "inmates," and the fines totaled about $18,000 per year paid in the police court.

The police regulation of the restricted district shows in the records of fines. The so-called underworld varied in population from 85 to 138 women, according to the number of fines reported. Nine persons paid fines of $50 each month for maintaining disorderly houses, except in the month of August, when only eight fines were reported, making a total of 107 arrests. The women inmates paid $10 a month, in most cases. Overall, a total of 1,333 arrests.[227]

For several months, the lights remained dark. No efforts were made to reopen the houses, although most of the inmates still lived there. By late April, the resorts had quietly reopened by using back door entrances.[228]

A few days after the reopening, the police raided the Midway, where Daisy Smith was taken, accused of running a house of ill fame, together with her four "guests" and two "inmates," Louise Brown, twenty-five, and Marion Grey. An hour later, the New Panama was raided, and Madam Nellie Lee, two guests and inmate Maxine Shaw arrested. The *Leader* reported:

As explained by the police, the old "line" has been operated a little more and more openly from the time since all were closed down, until recent weeks, when they became less guarded. The system was, the police have learned, for men to call up on the phone and gain entrance by rear doors while patrolmen watched the front entrances. In this manner, only the "friends" were admitted, to the exclusion of detectives. Many of the women have continued to live in the places, as private residences.[229]

A SENSATIONAL TRIAL THAT ENDED IN A WHIMPER

Insight into developments behind the scenes emerged during a sensational trial held in July 1917. The case was *State of Montana vs. Mrs. E.J. Nugent*, also known as Dorothy Hazzard, in which the latter was charged with conspiracy to bribe public officials. Over the course of the trial, Mayor A.J. Fousek provided blockbuster testimony that he was against closing Tenth Alley South and that he had quietly supported its reopening. Mayor Fousek knew the prostitution trade would continue, dispersed around the town, rather than in the orderly fashion it was operating under at Tenth Alley South. Many of the madams and other key players testified during the trial, revealing much about Tenth Alley South operations.

It took the jury in the Hazzard case just four hours to arrive at a verdict of not guilty. After many ballots, on a final vote of eight to four, Dorothy

Photo by Heyn.

Birdseye view showing one of important centers of Great Falls wholesale district at Tenth alley south. The latest additions to companies established here are the Loose-Wiles Biscuit company and the Overland-Great Falls Automobile company. The buildings at the center are all constructed of brick and well suited to become a busy jobbing and wholesale center.

Prostitution was closed down in Tenth Alley South in 1919, and the buildings found immediate use as a jobbing and wholesale center and detention hospital. *From the* Tribune, *September 21, 1919.*

Hazzard was found innocent of conspiracy to bribe public officials. She had been the leading influence in raising a fund aggregating $12,800 with which to "fix the officials" and thus reopen the district after it was closed in early January.[230]

TRANSFORMATION OF TENTH ALLEY SOUTH

Almost immediately, three of the alley's fine buildings were put to good use for critical joint city-county health needs, first against scarlet fever and smallpox and later the Spanish flu. Starting on December 25, 1917, when the detention hospitals of Tenth Alley South were rented, the city handled thirty-eight cases of smallpox and 116 cases of scarlet fever in the two hospitals, in addition to those cases in private homes. By June 1918, smallpox had been cleared out, and but a dozen cases of very mild scarlet fever remained in quarantine. However, soon after, the Spanish flu epidemic would strike. No. 126, the Ethel Warren House, became the scarlet fever detention hospital; No. 123, Bryant House, was the smallpox detention hospital; and No. 125, Warren House, served as the Spanish flu detention hospital.[231]

For many years, the buildings in Tenth Alley South housed commercial businesses, yet today no remnants of these buildings exist.

Chapter 20

LIBERTY THEATRE

On August 23, 1921, the Liberty Theatre opened at Central Avenue and Third Street to acclaim as "a jewel box." More than 3,600 attended the two opening night showings of *Nomads of the North*; another 2,000 were turned away. The opening nighters paid thirty cents; if they were children, ten cents. The first "talkie" was shown on August 29, 1928: the famed Al Jolson's *The Jazz Singer*. In October 1977, the lights went dark at the Liberty Theatre, although the classic building has been saved for reuse: the ground floor for retail stores and the upper floors for offices for the expanding D.A. Davidson Company.

LIBERTY OPENS

The Liberty was designed by premier architect George Shanley and constructed by Lease & Leighland. The three-story theater, prominently located on Central Avenue, was designed to be one of the most modern in the Northwest and the largest in Montana, with a seating capacity of 1,750. The Liberty became the pride of Great Falls.[232]

The *Tribune* heralded its opening on August 23, 1921, with the headline:

Liberty Theatre to Throw Open Its Doors Tonight
Great Falls' New Play House with $47,000 Wurlitzer Organ to Extend Welcome to Patrons

Brilliant Lighting Schemes, Both in Interior and Exterior, to Make Building Attractive; Comfort of People Is Provided For; "Nomads of the North" to Be First Picture Shown

The doors of the Liberty theater will be thrown open to the public this [Tuesday] *evening at 6:45 o'clock for the initial performance of the new playhouse. It will be under the management of E.J. Myrick, who opened the Rialto in Butte and has been in the employ of Jensen-Von Herberg* [of Seattle] *for a considerable length of time. Arnold D. Leverenz will be the organist. He has formerly played in the Coliseum and Liberty theaters in Seattle.*

No Expense Spared

Nothing has been spared to make the Liberty theater the most beautiful in Montana and the Pacific Northwest, according to the owners. More than $85,000 [almost $1.5 million today] *has been spent in furnishings alone and the immense Hope-Jones Wurlitzer unit organ cost $47,000....*

All interior lights will be concealed with red, white, and blue effects... made of ornamental plaster and polychromed wrought iron. Other lightings in the theater main will be operated by large dimmer which will enable them to start from a small glow and continue gradually until the full capacity is reached. Numerous lights will be concealed in a heavy cove.

Outside Lighting Brilliant

The outside lighting effect will be the equal of any of the numerous edifices of Jensen-Von Herberg. Stretched along a center line on the marquise will be six powerful flood lights which will make a great effect on the entire avenue. Each will be of 6,000 candle power. They will bring every detail of the terra cotta front with gorgeous effect. Many 100 candle power lights will spell the name of the theater....

Red Lights on Steam

Two large "burning torches" will glow from the top front of the building. The effect will be procured by a constant pouring of steam through the red-light effects. The main feature of the building lighting effects is the enormous Italian fountain sign which projects from the corner of the structure at Third street and Central avenue. Hundreds of colored lights will flash intermittently so as to make it difficult to distinguish it else than a regular flow of water from the fountain arrangement of more varied lights.

Designed by premier architect George Shanley, the Liberty Theatre opened to acclaim in 1921 as a "jewel box." *Author collection.*

Upholstering Is Heavy

What will interest the public is the construction of the 1,800 seats and loges. They were made to order by the Western Theater Equipment company. The loges are furnished with roomy reed chairs which are upholstered with soft velour cushions.

Color Scheme in Fawn Shades

The general color scheme is a soft blending of fawn shades and tiffany, and the ornamental plaster is tinted in primary colors, medium blue, orange, and American beauty effects. Although the general effect of coloring is a soft Nile tiffany not less than 50 different shades were used.

A radiant star of a gold eccentric mosaic background is the feature of the elaborate ceiling center piece.

A richly polychromed fruit border outlines on each side with heavy gold plaster effect, interwoven with ribbon forms the decorative feature of the stage opening. The main side wall panels have an elaborately hand painted design, the motif being ornaments griffins supporting a big medallion with hand painted figures which refer to the nine Muses of the drama.

The whole design and the panels are surrounded by an elaborate gold eccentric mosaic and the large pilasters which support the main cornice and

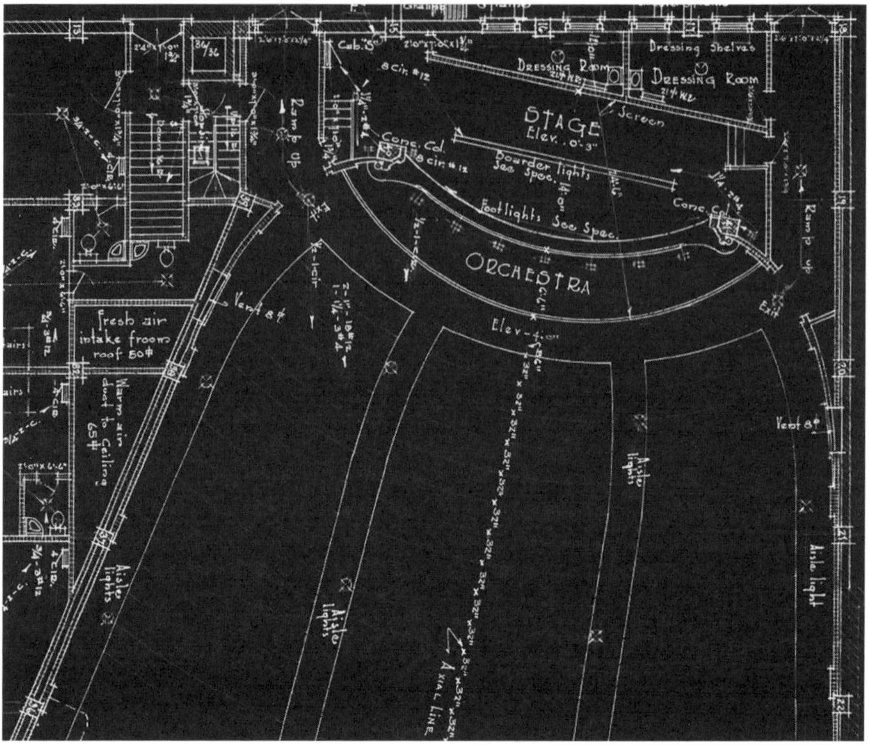

Blueprint of the Liberty Theatre's interior. *GF/CC HPO.*

coves are furnished with a burnished metallic effect. The two singers' boxes, high on each side of the stage, are richly colored with soft tiffany shades.

Rest Rooms Black and Red

The general rest rooms, both men's and ladies are hand painted to correspond with the gorgeous draperies and furnishings of each room. The color schemes for these compartments are black and Egyptian red and orange glazed chintz. It consists of draperies, portieres for the doors and furniture covers. The furniture is of French reed, painted in gold and surrounded with blue to correspond with the hangings. Several floor lamps are installed in the rooms, the shades of which are of parchment and varied silk shades which blend harmoniously with the general color scheme of the rooms.

"Gold Room" for Women

The women's rest room is designated as the "gold room" since each article has been carried out in gold effect. The carpets in the room are of two tones of gold, the elaborate hangings are of silk damask in the Louis XVI design and yellow and cream shades cover the windows. The furniture is of special design colored relative to the furnishings of the room.

Foyer and Aisles Carpeted

The foyer and ramps are carried out in harmony with the rest of the house, while the intermediate lobby has a wonderful hand-painted mural for its chief feature in the oval ceiling panel with the mythological figures which supported a gorgeously painted shield from which a large chandelier is hung.

The foyer and aisles throughout the floor arrangements will be covered with Bundahl imperial carpet, half an inch thick. The winding, gradually inclining runways which lead to the balcony are carpeted with the same material. Covering the floor of the main entrance will be a blue and orange Chinese rug.

Curtain Is Silk Damask

The main proscenium arch is draped with a large silk damask curtain and the upper part of the arch is covered with a big lambrequin of the same material with embroidered and painted motifs and cartouches. All this is so applied as to bring out the Italian Chippendale design which is used in effect throughout the theater. The large curtain is of a beautiful American beauty rose shade which is offset in a design of fawn color. Surfaced about one quarter of the height of the curtain from the bottom, is a stretched trimming of Roman gold tassels and fringes. Another, an inner curtain of pleated beautiful fawn colored satin is seen when the first drape is drawn back. With the brilliant effect of colored display lights played upon it, a most magnificent rainbow scene is made.

The third screen is disclosed when the first two are drawn back. This is the wonderful "movie" screen which Messrs. Jensen and Von Herberg have especially designed for the Great Falls theater, and no matter in what part of the house one sits, he may look directly at the picture as if he were in the center of the place.

The great [Wurlitzer] *organ was purchased at a cost of $47,000 for this Great Falls playhouse and was selected because it excels in sweetness of melody, as well as variety and beauty of effects produced. Indeed, so marvelous is its flexibility that it conveys the whole range of varieties from reproducing a great symphony orchestra to the tone of a fine church organ. The qualities of 40 instruments are considered in its orchestration. It requires 408,000 feet of electric wiring to give the organist full control of*

> *the many parts. The smallest pipe is no larger than a straw and the largest weighs 2,000 pounds.*
>
> *The feature on the program this* [opening] *night is James Oliver Curwoods "Nomads of the North," a story of the wilderness.*[233]

The next year, Charlie Russell and wife, Nancy, attended the Liberty to see Douglas Fairbanks in *The Three Musketeers*. The Russells had watched the film being made and had already seen the movie several times in California. Charlie pronounced it "a great picture."[234]

THE JAZZ SINGER

The Jazz Singer arrived in August 1928, bringing talkies to Great Falls. The Liberty outlaid $20,000, and a special crew of six men worked for ten days to install a new porous curtain to admit the passage of sound waves; behind this curtain were four six-hundred-pound amplifiers. On opening night, organists Arnold D. Leverenz and Roscoe Kernan provided sound effects on the magnificent Wurlitzer. The organists fit their music to what was on the screen: a tender interlude, a tense moment, a cavalry charge or a bomb burst.

The *Evening Leader* welcomed the advent of the talkies:

> *They are the realization of a dream, a thing impossible, yet ever true. Once upon a time the movie picture was a dream and after a while it also came true. But that the pictures could walk upon the screen and talk as in life—not, no never!*
>
> *Yet they do, and they do!*
>
> *The Vitaphone production of "The Jazz Singer" with Al Jolson—young as though born but yesterday—is a wonder, a heart twister, and picture of laughter and tears. The singing of Al Jolson is as if he were on stage in person, and one gasps in wonder.*[235]

During the Roaring Twenties, prices rose to fifty cents for adults, twenty-five for children and sixty for the loges. The Liberty offered continuous shows from one o'clock in the afternoon to eleven o'clock at night. Within a few years, the Great Depression hit, and the Liberty, along with other theaters, cut prices in January 1934 to thirty cents for "finer" main floor seats, twenty-five cents for balcony seats and ten cents for children. Those were the days when a child could go to the Liberty on Saturdays during Christmas vacation and other holidays by presenting a wrapper from a loaf of locally made "Eddy's bread."[236]

The Liberty Theatre and its rival in plush luxury, the Palace (formerly the Pantages Vaudeville Theater, later renamed the Rainbow), served the community well over the decades.

A Racial Incident

In the late 1940s, disturbing reports reached the Dunbar Art and Study Club at the Union Bethel African Methodist Episcopal Church that the Liberty's management was refusing to sell seats in the loges to African Americans. A Dunbar Club committee called on Will Steege, the Liberty's manager, to protest, and he promised the incident would not be repeated—and it was not.[237]

Shortly after, and perhaps because of that incident, Steege's Liberty showed the highly controversial, hard-hitting Darryl F. Zanuck "racial film" *No Way Out*—at the very time when Great Falls was beginning to confront discrimination against Black airmen at Great Falls Air Force Base as well as Black residents being informally but firmly restricted to housing on the lower Southside of town. Zanuck emphasized that earlier "Black theme" movies dealt only with the fringes of the problem, while *No Way Out*, starring Sidney Poitier, was the first film to show the full extent of the problems "the negro" was up against in daily life.[238]

New Owners

In July 1975, the Liberty Theatre and five other local theaters were sold to the Carisch Theater chain of Minneapolis. At that time, the Liberty Theatre building was home to Barnes Jewelry, Falls Barber Salon, RingsandThings Gift Shop and Travel Center, all fronting on Central Avenue, and the Liberty Shoe Shop, Liberty Barber Shop, Red Door Lounge, Teddy Jewelry and the Pantry Café on Third Street North.[239]

GOING DARK

The Liberty Theatre went dark after showing its last film, *The Hills Have Eyes*, on October 20, 1977. Owner Carisch Theaters announced tentative plans to convert the theater into a small retail mall, although this did not happen.[240]

LIBERTY CENTER

The Liberty Theatre building was sold again early in 1978, and its new owners considered razing it and replacing it with a seven-story office building. Fortunately, bad local economic conditions precluded this preservation loss. It was given a new name, Liberty Center, and architect Fritz Topel and contractor Palmer/Duncan Construction Company retained the exterior look and demolished the interior, developing an office building in its place.

The Liberty Theatre went dark in 1977, and today the building is the Liberty Center, an office complex. *Author photo.*

A central atrium stretched upward for more than fifty feet from the lower level, with skylights lighting the space. Retail offices filled the street level, while each of the three upper floors featured thirteen thousand square feet for offices.[241]

In a final step, in 1997, D.A. Davidson, chief executive officer of the D.A. Davidson Company, bought the Liberty Center and convinced the City of Great Falls to close one block of Third Street between the Davidson Company building and the Liberty Center. The Circle Plaza was installed west of the Davidson Building, featuring an outdoor amphitheater and a landscaped parking area. The Davidson building connects with the Liberty Center office and retail building via a ninety-foot glass pedestrian skywalk crossing Third Street, with the Davidson Courtyard below.[242]

Chapter 21

DEMPSEY INN

In 1893, the Volk brothers built a two-story stone residence during the years of the Volk Brewery. This stone building would have many lives. It was leased from the Volk family in 1914 and operated as the Park Saloon roadhouse in Great Falls Park on Upper River Road, then known as Lewis and Clark Drive. In the early 1920s, when the park was renamed Riverside Park, the roadhouse carried the same name. Heavyweight champion Jack Dempsey leased the complex from the Volks in May 1923 to serve as "Dempsey Camp" for six weeks while he trained for his most improbable heavyweight championship boxing bout against Tommy Gibbons in the little oil-boom town of Shelby, Montana. Dempsey used the home and park as his training headquarters. In the aftermath of that famed boxing match, the Dempsey name would remain when the roadhouse reopened as the Dempsey Inn. After Prohibition, the Dempsey Inn became a popular nightspot until it was partially destroyed by fire in 1966 and, later, demolished.

Descendant Charles E. Volk told the building's fascinating story to the *Tribune* under the headline:

Dempsey's Training Camp Well Worth 500 Bucks

On May 1, 1923, Jack Kearns, manager of Jack Dempsey, world heavyweight champion, signed an agreement in Chicago with Loy J. Molumby, commander of the Montana American Legion, for Dempsey to defend his crown against Tommy Gibbons of St. Paul, Minn. The fight

Leased from the Volk family in 1914, this building operated as the Park Saloon roadhouse in Great Falls Park until Prohibition. Jack Dempsey leased the complex from Christopher Volk as his training headquarters in 1923. The Dempsey name would remain when the roadhouse reopened as the Dempsey Inn. *THM.*

was to be at Shelby, a booming town due to the discovery of oil the previous year by Gordon Campbell.

The fight was to be July 4 with Dempsey receiving $300,000 plus $10 for expenses. The first $100,000 was to be paid on signing of the contract, the second $100,000 by June 16 and the final payment four days before the fight.

It had been two years since Dempsey had defended his title against Georges Carpentier of France at Jersey City, N.J., July 2, 1921. Dempsey, known as the "Manassas Mauler," won the title by knocking out Jess Willard at Toledo, Ohio, July 4, 1919.

Dempsey arrived to acclaim in Great Falls May 16, registered at the Park Hotel and immediately started looking for training quarters. Mayor Harry B. Mitchell and other dignitaries drove him around to several places and finally brought him to Great Falls Park, south of the city, where I was waiting.

Dempsey took one look at the area and asked how much it would cost to lease the place until July 10. It had been renting for $150 a month and, Dempsey being such a celebrity…so I asked for $500 for the period.

FIRST PICTURES OF CHAMPION IN GREAT FALLS QUARTERS

Here is the heavyweight king of the world, ready to start his Saturday afternoon workouts at Great Falls park. From left to right: Jack Burke, Pittsburgh heavyweight, Dempsey, Frank Powers, New York middleweight, and George Godfrey, giant colored sensation from Philadelphia.

The champion and his manager, Jack Kearns, standing outside the pavilion where Dempsey will do all his indoor training.

The first photos of champion Jack Dempsey after his arrival in Great Falls in May 1923. The photo on the left shows Dempsey with his sparring partners (*from left to right*): Jack Burke, Dempsey, Frank Powers and George Godfrey. The photo on the right shows champ Dempsey (*left*) with his manager, Jack Kearns. *Heyn & Keeley photo. From the* Tribune, *May 20, 1923.*

Dempsey handed me a $100 bill and asked me to come to the Park Hotel about 5 that evening and he would have an agreement ready to sign. He was in his shorts when I arrived and, frankly, he did not look all-powerful to me.

Dempsey moved out to the park the following day with his sparring partners and quartered in the large stone house. He arranged for construction of a 22-foot square ring in the dance hall with boxing dummies anchored to the ceiling. A second ring was to be constructed on the grassy slope next to the old brewery wall.

As a publicity stunt Dempsey visited the new livestock pavilion at the present fairgrounds and bought a bull.

Outside the fence surrounding Great Falls Park, my father had a log barn and a buggy shed. Dempsey asked me if he could use the buggy shed for a ticket office and the barn for his bull, to which I agreed with no charge.

He had a corral built against the barn and to this day I don't know who was photographed most—Dempsey or the bull.

Russell Strain of Strain Bros. asked me if he could place a billboard on the barn and I agreed.

Greedy Jack Kearns

On May 19, Kearns arrived in Great Falls and the atmosphere around the park changed immediately. Kearns closed all the fence openings and cut a new one opposite the ticket office. He collected a gate fee, sold concessions, picture rights, hot dogs, peanuts, and other items. He even installed a "Hit Me" charcoal blackface behind a canvas stretched over an arched doorway in the old brewery wall, using baseballs as missiles.

The gate and concessions netted him more than $8,000 during Dempsey's training period. Kearns asked Strain Bros. for $500 for their billboards rental but lost out on the deal when he was advised the ticket office and barn were outside the lease area.

Best Training Camp

Later Dempsey told me this was the most complete ideal training quarters he ever had. He said the last quarters he had, with hotel bills, cost him about $15,000. He said if I had asked that amount, he would have paid it. The location was ideal, secluded for early morning road work and yet close to town.

What did Dempsey get for his 500 bucks? It all started in June 1890 when Paris Gibson, founder of Great Falls, deeded to my father and uncle (Christian and Nicholas Volk), a plot of ground south of and adjoining Prospect Hill as the site for a brewery.

A stone quarry was opened on top of the hill immediately above the brewery location for building material....The brewery was constructed and had beer on the market in six months, Jun. 5, 1891....Shortly thereafter a beer garden was constructed adjoining the brewery. This garden was built around a large dance pavilion with a roofed observation platform on top....

A short distance west of the dance hall a saloon was built with an inside bar plus five bar openings to the outside, each protected by an eave overhang of six feet.

The gabled ends of the dance-hall observation platform and the saloon were ornamented with large cutouts depicting heads of the American Bald Eagle. The saloon was converted into a residence about 1931 and still stands as property of the park board. To the south of the pavilion were trapezes, horizontal bars, and swings. Trees, grass, and shrubs were planted, and the entire project enclosed by a high board fence.

In 1894 my dad built a nine-room cut-stone house on the high ground east of the dance pavilion. This was the Volk family residence for the next 20 years, later was known as Dempsey Inn. In 1896 the brewery was destroyed by fire.

Left: Cowboy Artist Charles M. Russell, an avid boxing fan, greeted world heavyweight champion Jack Dempsey at Great Falls Park. *Author collection.*

Below: Dempsey (*left*) sparring with Frank Powers at Great Falls Park. *Great Falls Photo View Co. Author collection.*

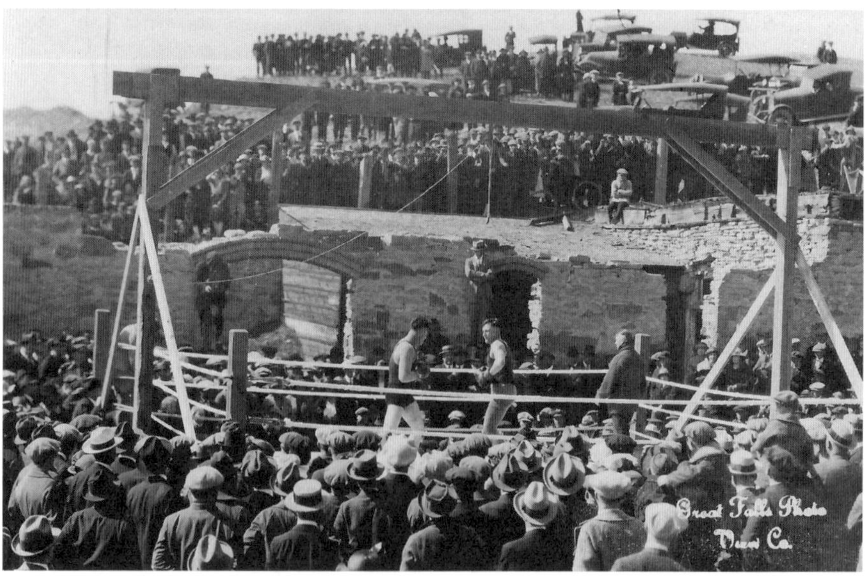

> *The beer garden, however, was maintained and operated and was known as Great Falls Park.... All this is what Dempsey leased. The only change was the high board fence enclosing the park. This had been replaced by a woven wire fence.*
>
> *In 1914 the park was leased by promoters of a roadhouse. A 15-room frame addition was built onto the stone house, so it could qualify for a hotel liquor license. Prohibition came in 1918 and the roadhouse was closed in 1920. Operating thereafter was a gambling casino until the Dempsey lease.*
>
> ***Popular Camp but Big Money Problems***
>
> *The Dempsey Camp was like a magnet, drawing crowds from far and near.*
>
> *On June 16, date of the scheduled second payment of $100,000 to Dempsey, sports fans were shocked to learn that James A. Johnson, mayor of Shelby and treasurer of the fight promotion organization had only $1,600 in the treasury.*
>
> *Kearns extended the deadline a few hours to allow local citizens to participate in an effort to raise the necessary money, which they did. George Stanton, Lee and Shirley Ford, Russell and Art Strain, Great Falls bankers and merchants, and Tip O'Neil, an oilfield operator and others saved the fight....* [Financing proved problematic to the very end; and the big bout almost did not happen.]
>
> *Kearns threatened to call the fight off and would have done it but for big-name sports reporters who had come to Montana to cover the training period and the fight. Early on the morning (3 a.m.) of July 3 Kearns agreed to hold the fight, having been given jurisdiction over the proceeds at the gate.*[243]

SAVING THE BOUT

According to a *Tribune* report, the following newspapermen were responsible for Kearns's decision to continue with the fight:

> *Grantland Rice, Lawrence Perry, Robert Edgren, Ernest Hopkins, and Damon Runyon added their arguments to those of others....*
>
> *For 60 days Shelby had been experiencing a fantastic boom. The arena, west of town, covering 33 acres, was enclosed by a board fence. The eight-sided wooden bowl itself covered six acres, being 558 feet across and had*

32 entrance gates. The arena was designed to seat 40,000 people. It was over a million board feet of lumber used in its construction.

The Great Northern Railroad had built three new depots, each with 1,000 feet of platform. Five miles of trackage was laid for the use of sleeping cars. The regular station was enlarged, and an addition was built to the eating house. One hundred special trains of 10 cars each were provided for. (All special trains from the East had been canceled by the end of June.)...

July 4, Wednesday, was hot and dusty and 7,966 persons passed through the gates as paid admissions. Kearns was $48,000 short on his final payment. Loss to the promoters and businessmen was about $80,000. Shelby losses, including Chamber of Commerce and concessionaires, totaled about $300,000.

Otto Floto of the Denver Post, *the West's best-known sports writer, told the* Tribune *the Shelby fight "was a wonderful exhibition. It seems a twist of fate that the Shelby battle with its small crowd should have turned into one of the greatest bouts on record."*

James Dougherty, the referee, said, "I think this will go down as one of the best heavyweight contests in all pugilistic history. It was the poorest arranged contest I ever witnessed and the best fight I ever saw in a championship contest."

Dempsey won 12 of the 15 rounds.[244]

THE DEMPSEY INN

In the aftermath of the great fight, less than two months later, Dempsey's training camp residence in Great Falls Park opened as the Dempsey Inn, advertising on August 25, 1923: "Grand Opening Dance Tonight. Good music. Good time. Good Floor. Entertainers also. Formerly Dempsey camp."[245]

Over the remaining decade of national Prohibition, the Dempsey Inn operated as a popular roadhouse, subject to occasional raids and abatement action for bootlegging and gambling.[246] More raids in 1930 led to its closing and reopening as the Tavern and, the next year, as the Alaska Café.[247]

The end of Prohibition brought the Dempsey Inn, with its name reestablished, back into action, and over the years, the inn proved a popular roadhouse destination. In December 1940, local hero Jack Dempsey returned to Great Falls and dined at the Dempsey Inn. A *Tribune* reporter interviewed the former champ under the headline:

Jack Dempsey Well Remembers Training Days in Great Falls

A flock of years have gone by, and a host of events have taken place since he trained here for his famous fight with Tommy Gibbons at Shelby in 1923 but Jack Dempsey, world heavyweight champion those days, recalls Montana as the place he was treated like royalty.

"Throughout my training days here, and the day we went to Shelby, everyone treated me like a royal friend, and I felt I was their friend," Dempsey said here Tuesday afternoon on the occasion of his first visit to Great Falls since the training days 17 years ago.

"Since that time, I have met hundreds of Montanans in New York and other places, and they have made me feel as though we were close friends. It's mighty nice to get back here again and renew some of those old acquaintances."

Dempsey appeared here Tuesday evening as referee at a boxing show in the civic center arena. Previously he was a guest at a dinner at Dempsey's Inn, a night club developed on the site of the champion's training site.

He recalled how he and his party were met at Helena in 1923 by Will Steege to make the train trip to this city. After arriving here and being greeted by a large delegation at the railway station, Dempsey said he immediately went into training in a serious way—but there were sidelights that came to mind in a hotel room here as he chatted with friends.

"Remember the dogs we had around camp?" he asked and then chuckled. "There were scads of them. Joe Benjamin had one that bit a girl one day and all sorts of trouble developed.

"Then there was that whiteface bull I bought and shipped to my friend Billy Lyons at Price, Utah. Billy was a boyhood friend of mine, and he wanted a fine whiteface from Montana to add to his herd.

"Oh yes, there was a wolf in our camp. Someone gave me a wolf and we kept him around for a while. One day it bit me, and somebody took the wolf away.

"I recall the time we went fishing at Charley Powers' place on Wolf creek. Boy, did we catch the fish. That was about the only time I got out of training camp here. I hadn't fought for two years, and I had a big job ahead getting in trim for Gibbons. It wasn't until about two days before the fight that I felt really in trim.

"Gibbons is now sheriff of Ramsey county in Minnesota and every time I go through there we get together and have a grand chat over old times and mutual friends. I saw him last about six months ago.

"There are a flock of Great Falls and Montana friends I recall. I often see Frank Walker and Frank Mencke in New York. Then there are other good friends I recall, such as Loy Molumby (deceased), Lee and Shirley Ford, Russ and Art Strain, Jim Flaherty, Frank O'Connell, Tip and John O'Neill, Dan Tracy, and Doc (E.M.) Porter, who was our camp physician. Of course, there were other friends I should recall to mind. Every minute I sit here I think of the names of more of them."…

Dempsey will leave this morning for Helena, where he will referee a fight card tonight.[248]

THE END OF DEMPSEY INN

October 1944 brought much-needed remodeling and redecorating to the Dempsey Inn. The following year, Christian and Annie Volk sold the five-acre property and buildings, including the Dempsey Inn, to William J. and Katherine M. Meier for $30,000.[249]

In the spring of 1962, the city bought three acres of the property to create Verde Park and enlarged it three years later.[250] By then, William Wong owned the Dempsey Inn. In June 1965, a fire caused extensive damage to the unoccupied second floor. The Dempsey Inn closed at that time.[251]

Two years later, Charles Volk, who was born there, nostalgically watched the walls come tumbling down. The end did not come easy for the seventy-four-year-old structure: its heavy beams and thick stone walls gave battle to the large tractor. With its demolition, the entire area became Verde Park, with not a one word of tribute to either the Volk past or Dempsey Camp.[252]

Chapter 22

OZARK CLUB

In 1896, a two-story wood-frame building was constructed at 116 Third Street South on the lower Southside. Over the following two-thirds of a century, that nondescript structure would evolve from a vice resort frequented by police raids into the legendary Ozark Club, the hottest jazz center between the Midwest and the West Coast, which attracted an interracial crowd and broke racial barriers.[253]

IN THE BEGINNING

During the early years, the nondescript wood-frame building's second floor, known as the Canada Rooming House, featured rooms for rent. The lower level ranged through a variety of businesses, such as the Great Falls Commission House, the Manila Café, R.E. Jones' Fruit and Confectionery store and R.E. Jones Cigars. Once Prohibition began, Dan Stafford opened a "soft drink parlor," featuring once or twice a year police raids and liquor violation charges. A typical police report found: "Three gallons of whisky, one case soft drinks, 24 bottles of soft drinks, nine quarts of soft drinks, five boxes of cigars."[254] Over the years, the upstairs rooms and residents of the Canada Rooming House were periodically raided as well. Charges ranged from selling opium and liquor to immoral behavior, adultery, vagrancy, keeping a disorderly house and maintaining a nuisance.[255]

During the final years of Prohibition, Ruth Spelias, who operated the Canada Rooming House, was indicted by a grand jury for sale and possession of liquor, although her fine of $300 was suspended with three years' probation.[256]

Meanwhile, George Diamont operated the former Stafford "Soft Drink Parlor" and was subject to raids by federal Prohibition agents J.Q. Adams and Burr Hill. Diamont was arrested and charged with illegal possession of liquor and operating a public nuisance.[257]

Twenty minutes after the dawn of the new year on January 1, 1933, a fire broke out in the rear of the unoccupied ground floor and spread quickly along partitions until it menaced the upstairs Canada Rooming House. Firemen brought the fire under control before the rooming house was harmed beyond smoke damage.[258] Two days later, another fire, believed to have been of incendiary origin, broke out in a bedroom in the rear of the second floor of the Canada Rooming House. While the flames were extinguished, more smoke and fire damage resulted.[259]

One minute after midnight on April 7, 1933, Prohibition ended in Montana. At the time, young Leo LaMar was working as a dining car waiter on the Havre to Butte run of the Great Northern Railway. Parlaying this experience, Leo opened a "colored only" Ozark nightclub in a small house at 413½ in Fourth Alley South, between Third and Fourth Streets. The next year, the O-Club, as it was known, moved to a larger, two-story building at 312½ Fifth Alley South.

By April 1935, the O-Club had moved again, this time to 914th Second Street South in the old Tenth Alley South district. Shortly after, the club was raided, and Leo LaMar was charged with obstructing a federal agent; the case was one of the first under a statute that laid down rules regarding federal officers entering a place where tax-paid goods were dispensed. LaMar demanded a preliminary hearing, and U.S. commissioner of revenue O.B. Kotz dismissed the charge.[260]

A FINAL LOCATION

Finally, in early December 1935, the Ozark Club moved to its final location at 116 Third Street South on the upper floor of the old wood-frame Canada Rooming House above the popular Alabama Chicken Shack Restaurant operated by Roger and Mary Berry. The Ozark Club, owned by the dynamic

Left: The Ozark Club in 1942, just as it was transforming from a "colored" club into the interracial jazz capital of Montana. *Author collection.*

Below: Ozark Boys, the famed house band at the Ozark Club, led by Bob Mabane (*center*). *Author collection.*

Leo LaMar, anchored Black nightlife in Great Falls for almost three decades. The O-Club achieved fame for its quality entertainment featuring some of the best Black jazz musicians in the country. In addition, Leo LaMar and his second wife, Beatrice Jeffers LaMar, achieved notoriety in the community for their involvement in gambling and operating a house of ill repute. There was never a dull moment in life at the Ozark Club.

ATTAINING JAZZ FAME

For three decades, from 1933 to 1962, the brightest spot in Montana's entertainment life was the unique Ozark Club on the lower Southside in Great Falls. The "O-Club" took on a life of its own: always lively, often magical and sometimes tragic.

The Ozark Club was located in the skid row district on the lower Southside in a building with a checkered past. Patrons climbed a long, narrow staircase to enter a dingy upstairs room with a bandstand on one end and a horseshoe-shaped bar on the other. Despite its simplicity, the Ozark Club sprang to life six nights a week with some of the hottest jazz music and entertainment between Chicago and the West Coast.

The Ozark Club reflected much of the character of its owners, Leo and his wife "Bea" LaMar. "Kid" Leo came to Great Falls as a teenage porter working for the Great Northern Railway. In the early 1920s, he gained local fame in American Legion boxing as a "tough as nails" lightweight. When Prohibition ended in 1933, Kid Leo opened the Ozark Club, serving a mainly African American clientele in a town with distinct racial boundaries for its small Black population.

World War II brought boom times to Great Falls. The Anaconda Smelter ran full-time copper production, and two army air corps bases filled the skies with lend-lease and bomber training aircraft and the streets of the town with thousands of servicemen. By May 1943, African American airmen had arrived at the bases, doubling the Black population overnight. In off-duty hours, these airmen sought entertainment, and since Black people were not welcome at the nightclubs and restaurants on Central Avenue, they found excitement and hot jazz at the Ozark Club.

This mosaic presents the amazing story of the Ozark Club. Dashing Leo LaMar (*left*) ran the whole operation: the club on the second floor, the café on the first floor, Woogie behind the bar and exceptional entertainment with hot jazz, torch singers and exotic dancers. The Ozark Club on the lower Southside of Great Falls was the "in" place and broke racial barriers in the 1940s and '50s. *LaMar family.*

BREAKING RACIAL BARRIERS

Everyone was welcome at the O-Club: Black and White, rich and poor, young and old. Leo LaMar opened his doors to all, breaking down racial barriers: only at the O-Club could Blacks and Whites mix and dance freely together. Through the 1940s, the club came to life with a distinctive entertainment package featuring live jazz music, torch singers and exotic dancers. The Ozark Boys combo was one of the finer small dance bands west of the Mississippi. Bob Mabane, on tenor sax, led the band, bringing his exceptional musical talent and the experience in jazz and bebop he'd gained in Kansas City playing with the famed Jay McShann orchestra, side by side with Charlie "Byrd" Parker.

As the years passed, Leo and Bea were able to attract a wide-ranging interracial crowd of patrons that included servicemen, traveling salesmen and couples looking for a good time. The combo players came and went, yet Bob Mabane remained, attracting top musicians such as Lionel Hampton, Oscar Dennard and Stan Turrentine. Added to the entertainment mix were star performers such as exotic dancer Miss Wiggles, torch singer Vivian Dandridge, comedian Redd Foxx and tap dancer Sneed Jackson. Sunday afternoon interracial jam sessions allowed young White alto sax player Jack Mahood and others to join the Ozark Boys. The O-Club's advertising in the *Great Falls Tribune* offered clever commentary on the times—taxes, elections, the space age, the Cold War and UFOs—to catch readers' attention.

OZARK CLUB LOST

But there was a dark side to the LaMars and the club. Beneath the surface was gambling in a back room and prostitution run by Bea at a hotel across the street. Tragedy struck in the late 1950s when their son Leo Jr. was killed in a car crash after his wife, Patricia, was mysteriously shot and killed. Leo Sr. died of a heart attack in June 1962, and the Ozark Club burned to the ground in a spectacular nighttime fire less than a month later. Just after midnight on July 12, firemen arrived on the scene to herd about fifty patrons and employees down the stairs to safety as the flames swept through the Ozark Club.

The famed Ozark Club ended in this blaze of glory. Great Falls lost its distinction as a "jazz capital"—and its magical interracial melting pot.

Right: Leo LaMar died of a heart attack on June 20, 1962. Three weeks later, just after midnight, firemen arrived on the scene and herded about fifty employees and patrons down the stairs and to safety as fire swept through the Ozark Club and Geiger's Repair Shop next door. Hot, tar-fed flames destroyed the famed club, bringing an end to the Great Falls "jazz capital" era. Rumors persist that the fire was arson. *Photo by Ray Ozmon. THM.*

Below: And the walls came tumbling down: Dick Olson Constructors demolished the remaining walls and rubble of the famed Ozark Club after the fire. *From the* Tribune, *July 27, 1962.*

Memories of the Ozark Club rose from the ashes through the words and recorded music of the elderly Jack Mahood in a series of oral history sessions with musician Phil Aaberg and the author at Fireside Books. Re-created Ozark Club excitement and jazz followed shortly after, in 2007, beginning a series of celebrations called A Night at the Ozark Club at The History Museum. Sixty-five years after the fiery end of the Ozark Club, one in four who came that first evening of live jazz in the new Ozark Room had been to the original Club, and they relived their fondest memories of very special evenings past. A packed house, young and old, Black and White, were welcomed, just as they had been at Leo LaMar's Ozark Club.[261]

Chapter 23

REQUIEM FOR FIRESIDE BOOKS

On October 1, 2005, the cultural lights of Great Falls dimmed as the lights went out at Fireside Books on 614 Central Avenue. On that day, Fireside Books closed its doors for business and Montana lost one of its finest antiquarian bookstores.

Fireside Books and its proprietor, Niel Hebertson, represented the best in antiquarian bookstores. Opened in 1993, the store—and its hardworking owner—quickly established a reputation around Montana as a friendly place for the discerning collector to find a rare book or the common reader to buy an inexpensive book to enjoy a good read.

Located in the one-story brick Ryan building on Central Avenue, Fireside Books brought people to downtown Great Falls. The Ryan building, built in the fall of 1925, opened in late December that year. Johnny's Market occupied the central 614 store. John J. Lauer and the Lauer family operated the market for two decades until it closed in May 1949. New businesses came and went over the next four decades, including the Montana Chemical Company, Mathews Royale Fashion Flair Wig School and Beauty Salon, Town & Country Fashions and Mathews Music Company. After retiring from the U.S. Air Force, Niel Hebertson opened Fireside Books at 614 Central in March 1993.[262]

Fireside was much more than a bookstore. It was an antiquarian bookstore in the finest tradition of that dying breed. Niel Hebertson was always the gracious host, offering a cup of coffee and a pleasant environment for casual or serious conversation. His time was your time. If your interest was sports,

Fireside Books, an exceptional antiquarian bookstore, closed its doors in 2005. *Author photo.*

that guided the conversation; a passionate hunter found a friend in Niel; your topic was his as you browsed the shelves or joined Niel at the big oak table. He knew and cared about rare books, but he also knew and cared about people.

A visit to Fireside had many dimensions. People came to buy a special present for a friend, looking through the fine offering of Montana history and Western Americana. They came to browse through a strong selection of children's books, admiring the old-style illustrations and covers that made yesterday's books for the young such a joy. They came to search through the extensive military selection that hinted at Niel's earlier career as an officer in the air force. Book dealers from around Montana and beyond stopped by Fireside to buy for their own stores, perhaps that special rare book or selections that Niel often had priced lower than their own. Writers and historians came to buy from Niel's fine selection and enjoy conversation with a knowledgeable bookman and Western history buff.

And then there were the regulars who came again and again to share a special friendship with both Niel and his bookshop. Always, Niel paused from his work at his computer, poured two cups of coffee—and the fun began.

Above: Fireside Books owner Niel Hebertson (*standing, left*), with Charles M. Russell scholar Brian Dippie displaying rare Russell books. *Author collection.*

Left: At the big oak table in Fireside Books, Jack Mahood related the dynamic story of the Ozark Club to the author and Montana musical treasure Phil Aaberg. In this photo (*from left*): the author, Jack Mahood and Phil Aaberg celebrate together at the first Night at the Ozark event at The History Museum. *Author collection.*

For Bob, the conversation might range from early Fort Benton to the latest find related to Lewis and Clark. For Mark, the topics would span military history and memorabilia. For Dwayne, the discussion might range from past military careers to collections of Montana political campaign ephemera. For Clint, the conversation compared hunting and fishing experiences. For Jack, the reminiscences might center on nightlife in Great Falls in the 1940s and '50s when he was a young, talented musician. With Ken, the topic du jour might relate to the latest historical nugget about early Great Falls found in dusty old newspapers at the public library or the latest historical treasure brought back to Montana from eBay. But always, the conversation would include the latest on families, wives and children.

And you met old and new friends at Fireside. Where else in Great Falls could you walk into a store, sit down at a big table with a cup of coffee and join a discussion with Hugh Dempsey, the great Canadian historian, or Brian Dippie, the fine Charlie Russell historian? Where else would you find Phil Aaberg, Montana's musical treasure, and this author jointly interviewing an elderly Jack Mahood about the early days of jazz in Great Falls at the uniquely important Ozark Club, where, as a young musician Jack jammed with some of America's finest Black jazzmen?

Yet today, the lights are out at Fireside Books. The coffee and conversations are but a delightful memory of the past. And we ask: why? The closure of Fireside came for several reasons. Great Falls is not a great bookman's town. For many, grabbing a used paperback at the Jungle or picking up a book at the Friends of the Public Library Book Sale will do. Walk-in traffic diminished over the years as many book collectors turned to the convenience of the Internet, finding their own selections online. And then there was the personal dimension. Several years ago, Niel tragically became a single parent to his four small children. For four years, he balanced raising his children with the demands of operating Fireside Books. In the end, it was simply too much. Whether we knew it or not, we all lost when the lights went out at Fireside Books.[263]

Chapter 24

THE BIG STACK

By the spring of 1909, Great Falls, the Electric City, had come a remarkable way in its twenty-five years. The arrival of the Great Northern in 1887 was followed, in rapid succession, by Black Eagle Dam; a silver smelter; the Boston & Montana Copper Smelter; silver mines in the nearby Little Belt Mountains; massive coal reserves at Belt and Sand Coulee; railroad repair yards; a second transcontinental railroad, the Milwaukee; and later in 1910, a second major dam at Rainbow Falls.

MONTANA'S STORY OF COPPER

Central to this rapid growth was the dramatic emergence of copper as the greatest treasure in Montana, the Treasure State. Copper that was mined in Butte, smelted in Anaconda and refined in Great Falls—that is Montana's "copper story." Copper that would "wire the world" in the early years of electricity and provide the armaments that would power the United States to victory in World War I and World War II rolled out of the refineries in Great Falls.

The *Leader* heralded the achievements of Great Falls, Montana's new industrial giant, as a notable new structure became operational—the biggest smokestack in the world.

GREAT FALLS DAILY TRIBUNE.

TWENTY-THIRD YEAR. GREAT FALLS, MONTANA, SUNDAY MORNING, JUNE 13, 1909. PRICE FIVE CENTS.

SMOKE ISSUES FROM BIG STACK

GONE TO BOTTOM

A Russian Submarine Goes Down, and All Hands Are Lost.

A "C.D.Q." RESCUE

A Big Ocean Steamer Stranded, but Passengers Saved.

HIGHEST CHIMNEY IN THE WORLD IS DOING BUSINESS

For the First Time Yesterday the Great Smoke Stack, That Has Attracted the Attention of the World, Was Used to Carry Away the Smoke From the Boston & Montana Smelter.

Height, 506 feet; diameter at bottom is 78 feet, at top, 50 feet inside.

(Continued on Page Two.)

NATIVE MUTINY

Filipino Constabulary Attack Officers. One American Is Killed.

GETTING AHEAD

Finish Second Reading Tariff Bill, Monday Will Start Third.

Top: Panoramic view of the Missouri River, Black Eagle Falls and the Boston & Montana Copper Smelter with its Big Stack. *Photo by Charles E. Morris. Author collection.*

Bottom: A front-page headline in the *Tribune* on June 13, 1909, heralded the operational status of the "Big Stack": at 506 feet, the tallest "chimney" in the world. *From the* Tribune, *June 13, 1909.*

The Great Falls Mascot

Great Falls has more resources than any city in the great northwest—but she has had them for many years past; she has the greatest water power in the world—but she has had that since the beginning of time; she has a surrounding farm country unsurpassed by any coal to burn, minerals to smelt and other things too numerous to mention—but all of them she has had since birth! Even her great smelter has been in business since 16 years ago, and her wheels of industry in other lines have been dusting for more or less time—all but the Big Stack!

For the Big Stack is the largest thing of its kind in the entire world—and it is an eighth wonder of the world—standing 506 feet from base to top—with 50 feet inside diameter at the upper opening—with the opening 1,200 feet higher than the furnaces below—with a draft equal to carrying a man up and shooting him from the top like a bean straw—a modern marvel of engineering wonder and it's no wonder that the world wonders, and that in the way of a mascot the Big Stack is something wonderful!

Every resource of Great Falls was in place long before the Big Stack, but it took that great industrial exclamation point to focus the spotlight properly; with such a mascot, accomplishing such results even from the first brick, what will happened when the smoke begins to pour out can hardly be overestimated by the most enthusiastic.

As a real, up-to-date mascot, the Big Stack is the Big Smoke—and the only one of its kind in the world. No wonder that Great Falls is being heralded from one end of the country to the other as the real goods, that investors are heading in on the spur of the Big Stack, [that] *homeseekers are falling all over themselves to homeseek, that railroads are battling for the low places, and land prosperity is beginning to hit the high places.*

Besides peddling out smoke amongst the streets of stars, and smoking collars out amongst an appreciative people, from here to the Big Stack on the summit of Indian Point stands also the Great Falls mascot of industrial, financial, and advertising uplift—the awakening alarm bell of the big sleep—the industrial spotlight in the lighthouse of prosperity.

It is not the things which the Big Stack stands for directly, but the things to which the Big Stack gives direction that count, and therein the work of the Big Stack as a Great Falls mascot stands out as the real thing in mascots—the best in the business.

And the business is getting better all the time![264]

COSTLY CONSTRUCTION

The contract for building the massive smokestack went to Alphons Custodis Construction Company of New York. The foundation was laid, a rail line was put in place and a brick-making plant was constructed, capable of producing an astounding 120 tons of perforated radial bricks per day. The first brick went in place on April 7, 1908. Three months later, worker Ralph Jones slipped from scaffolding and fell 180 feet to his death. The last brick was laid on October 23, and a second worker, Peter C. Yeager, fell 220 feet, victim to the giant project, when helping to remove scaffolding from the interior of the stack.[265]

OPERATIONAL

On June 12, 1909, the Big Stack became operational, carrying away the gases, fumes and smoke from the Boston & Montana (later to become the Anaconda) Smelter. The smokestack would have the immense duty of carrying off four million cubic feet of gases every minute, consisting of mainly sulfuric acid fumes.[266]

The Big Stack became an instant landmark, visible through the wheat fields for many miles as cars approached Great Falls from every direction. *Author collection.*

The smokestack was 506 feet in height; 17,000 tons of brick were used in its construction; and it was engineered to withstand winds of 120 miles per hour. The Washington Monument, which is fifty feet square at the bottom and twenty feet square at the top, could be set inside the Big Stack without touching any wall—and there would still be room between the walls of the chimney and the monument to drive a span of horses from top to bottom. Such was the scale of the tallest and largest chimney in the world.[267]

FROM MASCOT TO LANDMARK SYMBOL OF GREAT FALLS

As sixty-three years passed by, the big chimney continued operations—although its height was overtaken by that of the Washoe Smelter Stack at Anaconda in 1918. The Big Stack, begun as a mascot, evolved into an historical landmark, the symbol of Great Falls and its industrial history and a monument to its people, past and present. Visible for many miles from every direction on the compass, the Big Stack rose as a destination landmark for motorists approaching the Electric City.

In 1972, the Anaconda Copper Company fell on hard times and closed its zinc refinery in Great Falls, and the Big Stack stopped smoking. Clouds had been on the horizon for some years. Repairs were made in the mid-1950s, including the installation of more than one hundred iron straps circling the chimney. In 1959, the interior brickwork was crumbling and deteriorating seriously, and the Custodis Construction Company returned for repairs. The bands were removed in 1976 for use in strengthening the Anaconda Stack. Anaconda sold the Great Falls smelter to Atlantic Richfield Company (ARCO), which then closed the copper refinery in September 1980.[268]

The end was nearing for the Big Stack. ARCO determined it was unstable and scheduled its demolition along with the one hundred buildings on the company's closed industrial site. In 1981, Hungarian refugee Greg Kecskes, who "fell in love" with Great Falls in 1969 when he first arrived there with the U.S. Air Force, launched a one-man "SOS" campaign to "Save Our Stack." Kecskes announced, "To me, history is culture. And if we have no history, we have no culture....It is one of the few things left of the original Great Falls."[269]

Though the SOS campaign pressed forward and many in the community rallied in support, they were unable to raise the \$350,000–\$500,000 necessary to save and repair the Big Stack. Demolition was scheduled for September 18, 1982, and no sentiment or legal maneuvering could stop it—only big money, and that was not to be.[270]

The Death of the Big Stack

On a sunny Saturday, September 18, the *Tribune*'s Richard Ecke set the woeful scene:

> *They brought their dogs, kids, cameras, cowboy hats, soccer balls and blankets.*
>
> *But they didn't bring much cheer with them….*
>
> *Up on Wire Mill Road, Gerry Smith hadn't brought his girlfriend with him. She wouldn't come.*
>
> *"She thinks it's just like watching somebody die," he said….*
>
> *Mostly it was quiet, as many stayed in their cars. Others spread out along a sloping field.*
>
> *Then they waited.*
>
> *Just like clockwork, the Simmons oil refinery siren sounded at 10:05 a.m. Five minutes later, dynamite exploded. And the stack fell to rubble—almost.*
>
> *Standing erect after the smoke cleared was a large sliver of stack, looking like a broken pastry shell.*
>
> *Many in the crowd hooted and clapped.*
>
> *It was a fitting near-end to the stack. To many, it confirmed suspicions that the stack was a lot stronger than the experts were saying.*
>
> *Bitterness and cynicism were common. And underneath it all was a general feeling of helplessness.*
>
> *"I love the stack and they blew it," said Bing Cosby later that afternoon at Collins Park in Black Eagle….*
>
> *By evening, the demolition crew had finally finished off the stack and a scaled-back crowd lingered for a moment.*
>
> *"That's it," one man said.*
>
> *And there was nothing more to say.*[271]

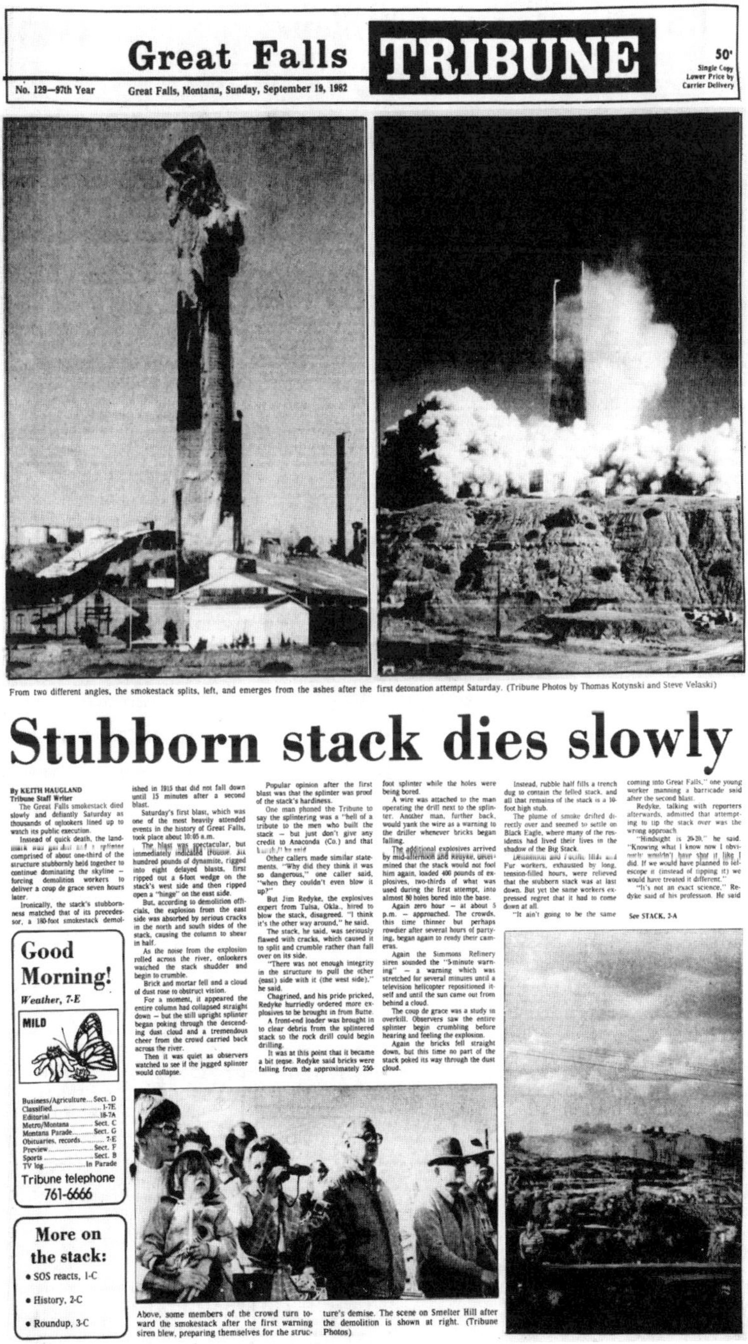

Great Falls TRIBUNE

50¢ Single Copy Lower Price by Carrier Delivery

No. 129—97th Year Great Falls, Montana, Sunday, September 19, 1982

From two different angles, the smokestack splits, left, and emerges from the ashes after the first detonation attempt Saturday. (Tribune Photos by Thomas Kotynski and Steve Velaski)

Stubborn stack dies slowly

By KEITH HAUGLAND
Tribune Staff Writer

The Great Falls smokestack died slowly and defiantly Saturday as thousands of onlookers lined up to watch its public execution.

Instead of quick death, the landmark was [illegible] and a splinter comprised of about one-third of the structure stubbornly held together to continue dominating the skyline — forcing demolition workers to deliver a coup de grace seven hours later.

Ironically, the stack's stubbornness matched that of its predecessor, a 180-foot smokestack demolished in 1915 that did not fall down until 15 minutes after a second blast.

Saturday's first blast, which was one of the most heavily attended events in the history of Great Falls, took place about 10:05 a.m.

The blast was spectacular, but immediately indicated trouble. Six hundred pounds of dynamite, rigged into eight delayed blasts, first ripped out a 6-foot wedge on the stack's west side and then ripped open a "hinge" on the east side.

But, according to demolition officials, the explosion from the east side was absorbed by serious cracks in the north and south sides of the stack, causing the column to shear in half.

As the noise from the explosion rolled across the river, onlookers watched the stack shudder and begin to crumble.

Brick and mortar fell and a cloud of dust rose to obstruct vision.

For a moment, it appeared the entire column had collapsed straight down — but the still upright splinter began poking through the descending dust cloud and a tremendous cheer from the crowd carried back across the river.

Then it was quiet as observers watched to see if the jagged splinter would collapse.

Popular opinion after the first blast was that the splinter was proof of the stack's hardiness.

One man phoned the Tribune to say the splintering was a "hell of a tribute to the men who built the stack — but just don't give any credit to Anaconda (Co.) and that [illegible]," he said.

Other callers made similar statements. "Why did they think it was so dangerous," one caller said, "when they couldn't even blow it up?"

But Jim Redyke, the explosives expert from Tulsa, Okla., hired to blow the stack, disagreed. "I think it's the other way around," he said.

The stack, he said, was seriously flawed with cracks, which caused it to split and crumble rather than fall over on its side.

"There was not enough integrity in the structure to pull the other (east) side with it (the west side)," he said.

Chagrined, and his pride pricked, Redyke hurriedly ordered more explosives to be brought in from Butte.

A front-end loader was brought in to clear debris from the splintered stack so the rock drill could begin drilling.

It was at this point that it became a bit tense. Redyke said bricks were falling from the approximately 250-foot splinter while the holes were being bored.

A wire was attached to the man operating the drill next to the splinter. Another man, further back, would yank the wire as a warning to the driller whenever bricks began falling.

The additional explosives arrived by mid-afternoon and Redyke, determined that the stack would not fool him again, loaded 400 pounds of explosives, two-thirds of what was used during the first attempt, into almost 80 holes bored into the base.

Again zero hour — at about 5 p.m. — approached. The crowds, this time thinner but perhaps rowdier after several hours of partying, began again to ready their cameras.

Again the Simmons Refinery siren sounded the "5-minute warning" — a warning which was stretched for several minutes until a television helicopter repositioned itself and until the sun came out from behind a cloud.

The coup de grace was a study in overkill. Observers saw the entire splinter begin crumbling before hearing and feeling the explosion.

Again the bricks fell straight down, but this time no part of the stack poked its way through the dust cloud.

Instead, rubble half fills a trench dug to contain the felled stack, and all that remains of the stack is a 10-foot high stub.

The plume of smoke drifted directly over and seemed to settle on Black Eagle, where many of the residents had lived their lives in the shadow of the Big Stack.

[illegible] Fur workers, exhausted by long, tension-filled hours, were relieved that the stubborn stack was at last down. But yet the same workers expressed regret that it had to come down at all.

"It ain't going to be the same coming into Great Falls," one young worker manning a barricade said after the second blast.

Redyke, talking with reporters afterwards, admitted that attempting to tip the stack over was the wrong approach.

"Hindsight is 20-20," he said. "Knowing what I know now I obviously wouldn't have shot it like I did. If we would have planned to telescope it (instead of tipping it) we would have treated it different."

"It's not an exact science," Redyke said of his profession. He said

See STACK, 2-A

Good Morning!

Weather, 7-E

MILD

Business/Agriculture	Sect. D
Classified	1-7E
Editorial	18-7A
Metro/Montana	Sect. C
Montana Parade	Sect. G
Obituaries, records	7-E
Preview	Sect. F
Sports	Sect. B
TV log	In Parade

Tribune telephone 761-6666

More on the stack:

- SOS reacts, 1-C
- History, 2-C
- Roundup, 3-C

Above, some members of the crowd turn toward the smokestack after the first warning siren blew, preparing themselves for the structure's demise. The scene on Smelter Hill after the demolition is shown at right. (Tribune Photos)

The mighty Big Stack proved a demolition challenge. *From the* Tribune, *September 19, 1982.*

Demolition of the Big Stack in action. *From the* Tribune, *"The Big Stack."*

THE MEANING

Through the eyes and tears of many thousands of Great Falls residents, the Big Stack died slowly and defiantly that Saturday afternoon. The public execution of this beloved landmark not only symbolically ended Great Falls' industrial era, but it also knocked the wind out of the community's sails for decades to come. The loss of thousands of jobs triggered a downward economic spiral, coupled, sadly, with a devastating blow to community spirit. The Big Stack, the mascot that became a historical landmark, the symbol of Great Falls, was lost.

NOTES

Chapter 1

1. First Peoples Buffalo Jump State Park, https://montanakids.com/things_to_see_and_do/state_parks/ulm.htm.
2. *Great Falls Tribune* (hereafter *Tribune*), March 25, 1984.
3. *Tribune*, September 29, 1973.

Chapter 2

4. Works Progress Administration, *Great Falls Yesterday*, viii.
5. *Sun River Sun*, April 10, 1884.
6. Works Progress Administration, *Great Falls Yesterday*, viii.
7. Ibid., 323.
8. *Sun River Sun*, June 12, 1884; Works Progress Administration, *Great Falls Yesterday*, 19, 131; Cheney, *Names on the Face of Montana*, 125.
9. *Great Falls Leader* (hereafter *Leader*), August 18, 1928.
10. *Tribune*, October 3, 1885.
11. *Tribune*, October 9, 1886.
12. *Leader*, November 7, 1891.

Chapter 3

13. *Great Falls Public Schools 100th Anniversary*, 1.
14. Great Falls High School, *The Round-Up 1923*, 82.

15. *Tribune*, June 25, August 8 and September 12, 1885.
16. James Marion Largent was born in 1855 in Iowa. He married Neoma Lease Crawford in 1875 and moved to Great Falls as it was formed. A Disciples of Christ minister, Largent died of pneumonia in Augusta in 1894. *Tribune*, September 12, 1885.
17. *Tribune*, October 24, 1885.
18. *Tribune Weekly*, November 21, 1885.
19. *Tribune*, October 24, 1885.
20. *Tribune*, December 20, 1903.
21. *Tribune*, January 2, 1886.
22. *Tribune Weekly*, August 24, October 9 and November 5, 1887.
23. *Great Falls Public Schools 100th Anniversary*, 2.
24. *Tribune*, January 16, 1888; *Tribune Weekly*, September 29, 1888.
25. *Leader*, May 15, August 28 and September 11, 1889.
26. *Tribune Weekly*, May 5, 1893; *Leader*, April 7, 1901.
27. *Tribune*, December 4, 1977, and January 4, 1978.
28. *Tribune*, August 21, 1978.
29. *Tribune*, August 25, 1979, and March 18, 1980.

Chapter 4

30. *Tribune*, November 14, 1887.
31. Ibid.
32. Through an act of ignorance, the first territorial legislature misspelled the county's name, and it was not corrected to Chouteau until a legislative act in 1903.
33. Works Progress Administration, *Great Falls Yesterday*, xi.
34. *Tribune*, November 22, 1888.
35. *Tribune*, January 12, 1888.
36. *Tribune*, February 22, 1888.
37. *Tribune*, June 1 and December 11, 1888.
38. *Tribune*, July 31, 1890.
39. *Leader*, September 9, 1890.
40. *Leader*, September 18, 1890.
41. *Leader*, October 7, 1890.
42. *Leader*, October 16, 1890.
43. *Leader*, October 21, 1890.
44. *Tribune Weekly*, November 2, 1894.
45. *Tribune Weekly*, November 23, 1894.
46. *Tribune*, March 30, 1919.
47. *Tribune*, October 24, 1982, and October 10, 1985.

Chapter 5

48. *Tribune*, June 20, 1889
49. *Tribune*, December 17, 1911.
50. *Tribune*, June 20, 1889.
51. *Tribune*, August 28, 1889.
52. *Tribune Weekly*, March 26, 1892.
53. *Tribune Weekly*, November 23, 1894.

Chapter 6

54. *Tribune Weekly*, November 13 and 20, 1886.
55. *Tribune*, May 4, 1889.
56. *Tribune Semiweekly*, August 7 and November 22, 1889.
57. *Tribune Weekly*, October 23, 1889.
58. *Leader*, December 18, 1889.
59. *Tribune Semiweekly*, January 22, 1890; *Leader*, September 19, 1890.
60. *Tribune Semiweekly*, October 4, 1890; *Leader*, October 17, 1890.
61. *Tribune*, October 18, 1890.
62. *Tribune Weekly*, March 14, 1891.
63. *Tribune*, February 20, 1891, and January 28, 1894.
64. *Leader*, February 9, April 4 and April 29, 1892.
65. *Leader*, November 12, 1896.
66. *Tribune*, December 17, 1911; February 8, 1919; and January 4, 1921.
67. *Tribune*, September 22, 1962.

Chapter 7

68. *Tribune*, October 3, 1890.
69. *Leader*, January 29 and February 22, 1890; *Tribune*, May 26, 1963.
70. *Tribune*, August 16, 1890, and May 26, 1963.
71. *Tribune*, May 26, 1963, and October 11, 1890.
72. *Tribune*, May 26, 1963.
73. Vrooman, *Whole Country*, 274.
74. *Leader*, June 22, 1896.
75. *Tribune*, May 26, 1963.
76. *Tribune*, June 9, 1901.
77. Ibid.
78. *Tribune*, May 26, 1963.
79. *Leader*, January 3, 1903.

Chapter 8

80. *Leader*, July 31, 1890.
81. *Tribune*, August 31, 1890.
82. *Leader*, March 17, 1891; *Tribune*, February 22, 1891.
83. *Tribune*, November 25, 1931.
84. *Tribune*, November 30, 1931.

Chapter 9

85. *Tribune*, June 12, 1890.
86. *Leader*, October 29, 1890.
87. *Tribune*, December 25, 1890.
88. *Tribune*, June 7, 1893.
89. *Tribune Weekly*, June 30, 1893.
90. *Tribune*, June 3, June 30 and July 21, 1893, and October 9, 1894.
91. *Tribune*, July 4 and July 6, 1894.
92. *Leader Weekly*, October 29, 1896; *Leader*, July 2, 1935.
93. *Tribune*, March 9, 1967.

Chapter 10

94. *Leader*, February 20, 1891.
95. *Leader*, April 24 and May 2, 1891.
96. *Tribune Semiweekly*, June 27, 1891.
97. *Leader Weekly*, July 2, 1891.
98. *Tribune*, September 29, 1891.
99. *Tribune*, October 21, 1891.
100. *Leader*, January 4, 1892.
101. *Tribune*, January 5, 1892.
102. *Leader*, August 1, 1895.
103. *Leader*, August 6, 1895.
104. *Tribune*, March 11, 1906.
105. *Leader*, October 30, 1906.
106. *Tribune*, June 21, 1955.

Chapter 11

107. For a list of members of the Electric City Club, see www.kenrobisonhostory.com/LOST-GF; *Tribune*, November 23, 1894.

108. *Tribune*, November 23, 1894.
109. *Anaconda Standard*, August 2, 1895.
110. *Leader*, August 1, 1895.
111. *Tribune*, August 27, 1906.
112. *Leader*, April 29, 1908.
113. *Tribune*, March 30, 1919.
114. *Tribune*, April 3, 1919.

Chapter 12

115. *Tribune*, May 9, 1897.
116. *Tribune*, July 4, 1897.
117. *Tribune*, November 22, 1898.
118. *Leader*, June 22, 1900.
119. Joe Tinker became a key part of one of the best ever major leagues double play combinations, immortalized in the poem "Tinker to Evers to Chance." For the story of Tinker's short but memorable career in Great Falls, see www.kenrobisonhostory.com/LOST-GF.
120. *Tribune*, November 13, 1900.
121. Ibid.
122. Ten young women, representing seven Indian nations, formed the Fort Shaw girls' basketball team that not only dominated Montana basketball in the early 1900s but also went on to triumph nationally in St. Louis in 1904. Their forgotten story is told by Linda Peavy and Ursula Smith in *Full-Court Quest*.
123. *Tribune*, June 27, 1903.
124. *Leader*, July 13, 1903.
125. *Leader*, August 13, 1903.
126. *Tribune*, August 20, 1904.
127. *Tribune*, September 25, 1904.
128. *Tribune*, September 26, 1904.
129. *Leader*, September 26 and 27, 1904.
130. *Tribune*, June 17, 1911.
131. *Tribune*, March 10 and April 30, 1938.

Chapter 13

132. *Tribune*, April 30, 1888; *Leader*, August 18, 1928; *Leader Weekly*, June 16, 1888.
133. *Tribune*, July 7, 1888.
134. *Leader*, March 22, 1892.
135. *Tribune*, February 11, 1900.
136. *Tribune*, August 17, 1900.

137. *Leader*, January 1, 1901.
138. *Tribune*, February 13, 1901.
139. *Leader*, February 14, 1901.
140. Peavy and Smith, *Full-Court Quest*, 64–67.
141. *Leader*, January 16, 1903. For more about the Fort Shaw girls' basketball team, see www.kenrobisonhistory.com/LOST-GF.
142. *Tribune*, October 17, 1909; February 27, 1911; and July 26, 1916.
143. *Leader*, December 13, 1919.
144. *Tribune*, August 28, 1927.
145. *Tribune*, September 25, 1931.
146. *Tribune*, November 17, 1965.
147. *Tribune*, June 8, 2000.

Chapter 14

148. *Tribune*, December 8, 1918.
149. *Tribune*, December 31, 1918.
150. *Tribune*, February 1 and March 27, 1919.
151. *Leader*, April 16, 1927.
152. *Leader*, September 23, 1911, and April 16, 1927; *Tribune*, January 20, 1989.
153. *Tribune*, July 4, 1932.
154. *Tribune*, September 23, 1953.
155. *Tribune*, October 24, 1982.

Chapter 15

156. *Tribune*, December 8, 1918.
157. *Leader*, November 25, 1899, and June 17, 1896.
158. *Leader*, May 8, 1907.
159. *Leader*, January 19, 1928.
160. *Tribune*, March 8, 1919.
161. Montgomery, *Years of George Montgomery*, 26.
162. *Leader*, June 16, 1948.
163. *Tribune*, April 5, 1948.
164. *Leader*, June 18, 1948.
165. *Leader*, November 30, 1948.
166. *Tribune*, December 21, 1948.
167. *Tribune*, February 10, 1949.
168. *Tribune*, April 1, 1949.
169. *Tribune*, May 9, 1951.
170. *Tribune*, March 14, 1952.

171. *Tribune*, August 27, 1952; Remick, "Myth Is Punctured."
172. *Tribune*, April 23, April 26 and May 8, 1967.

Chapter 16

173. *Leader*, July 3, 1906.
174. *Tribune*, June 7, 1906.
175. *Leader*, August 4, 1906.
176. *Tribune*, July 8, 1906.
177. *Leader*, June 1, 1907.
178. *Tribune*, July 31, 1908.
179. *Leader*, May 25, 1909.
180. *Leader*, June 21, 1911; *Tribune*, August 16, 1911.
181. *Tribune*, October 25, 1912.
182. *Leader*, September 23, 1915.
183. *Tribune*, June 3, 1914.
184. *Leader*, October 12, 1920.
185. *Tribune*, March 14, 1922.
186. *Leader*, March 15, 1922.
187. *Leader*, November 10, 1923.
188. *Tribune*, August 24, 1919.

Chapter 17

189. *Leader*, May 31, 1910.
190. *Tribune*, December 12, 1888.
191. *Tribune*, June 22, 1910.
192. *Tribune*, November 16, 1913.
193. *Tribune*, October 24, 1982.
194. *Tribune*, November 17, 1963.

Chapter 18

195. *Leader*, August 1, 1914.
196. *Tribune*, August 2, 1914.
197. Russell, "Pantages Theater."
198. *Tribune*, August 2, 1914.
199. Ibid.
200. Ibid.
201. Ibid.
202. *Tribune*, August 11, 1914.

203. *Leader*, August 11, 1914.
204. *Tribune*, May 8 and June 30, 1915.
205. *Tribune*, March 13, 1926, and May 25, 1966.
206. *Tribune*, January 14, 1966.

Chapter 19

207. This document by John Stevenson Sr. was found by the author in the vertical files in the Montana Room at the Great Falls Public Library. Jay Moynahan's *Red Light Revelations* presents many newspaper articles related to prostitution in Great Falls between 1889 and 1918—including many provided to him by this author.
208. *Tribune*, June 20, 1914.
209. *Leader*, November 20, 1913; *Tribune*, June 20, 1914.
210. *Leader*, February 16, 1915.
211. *Tribune*, November 30, 1913.
212. *Tribune*, May 27, 1914.
213. *Tribune*, June 5, 1917.
214. *Tribune*, May 27, 1913; *Leader*, December 22, 1917.
215. *Tribune*, March 13, 1919.
216. *Leader*, February 26, 1914.
217. *Tribune*, May 27, 1914.
218. *Leader*, July 2, 1914.
219. *Leader*, November 20, 1913.
220. *Leader*, August 1, 1913; *Tribune*, April 4, 1914.
221. *Tribune*, October 24, 1913.
222. *Leader*, August 30, 1913.
223. *Tribune*, March 13, 1919.
224. *Tribune*, May 27, 1913.
225. *Tribune*, December 22, 1917.
226. *Leader*, January 9, 1915.
227. *Leader*, January 8, 1917.
228. *Leader*, January 12, 1917.
229. *Leader*, April 21, 1917.
230. *Tribune*, July 22, 1917.
231. *Tribune*, March 5, June 7 and October 14, 1918.

Chapter 20

232. *Tribune*, August 23, 1921.
233. Ibid.
234. *Leader*, June 3, 1922.
235. *Leader*, August 30, 1928.

236. *Tribune*, October 23, 1977.
237. MHS, MC281/1/12.
238. *Leader*, December 16, 1950.
239. *Tribune*, July 27, 1975.
240. *Tribune*, October 21, 1977.
241. *Tribune*, June 27, 1982.
242. *Tribune*, August 19, 1997, and January 26, 1998.

Chapter 21

243. *Tribune*, July 1, 1973.
244. *Leader*, July 4, 1923.
245. *Tribune*, August 25, 1923.
246. *Tribune*, April 14, 1929; *Leader*, November 6, 1929.
247. *Leader*, May 9, 1930; *Tribune*, August 22, 1931.
248. *Tribune*, December 4, 1940.
249. *Leader*, October 2, 1944; *Tribune*, December 7, 1945.
250. *Tribune*, August 6, 1965.
251. *Tribune*, June 22, 1965.
252. *Tribune*, September 3, 1967.

Chapter 22

253. For the dramatic story of the Ozark Club and the special role played by its owner, Leo LaMar, in Great Falls, see Ken Robison, "Breaking Racial Barriers: 'Everyone's Welcome' at the Ozark Club Great Falls, Montana's African American Nightclub," in *Montana: A Cultural Medley*, ed. Robert R. Swartout Jr., 350–76.
254. *Leader*, April 2, 1924.
255. *Leader*, December 30, 1923; January 9, 1924; July 26, 1926; February 13, 1928; and October 4, 1930.
256. *Tribune*, April 22 and 26, 1931.
257. *Leader*, August 23 and October 15, 1932.
258. *Tribune*, January 1, 1933.
259. *Tribune*, January 4, 1933.
260. *Tribune*, January 4, 1933.
261. This short account of the Ozark Club is derived from "Breaking Racial Barriers."

Chapter 23

262. *Great Falls City Directories*; *Leader*, August 4 and December 10, 1925; *Tribune*, May 13, 1949, and May 4, 1970.

263. As the local economy has rebounded from the 1980s industrial closures and downtown Great Falls has undergone a dramatic resurgence, an independent bookstore, Cassiopeia Books, has opened its doors.

Chapter 24

264. *Leader*, April 24, 1909.
265. Carlcaburu, *Big Stack*, 37–38.
266. Ibid.
267. Ibid.
268. Ibid.
269. *Tribune*, November 21, 1981.
270. Ibid.
271. Carlcaburu, *Big Stack*, 11.

BIBLIOGRAPHY

Online Resources

First Peoples Buffalo Jump State Park. https://montanakids.com/things_to_see_and_do/state_parks/ulm.htm.

Ken Robison History. http://www.kenrobisonhostory.com/LOST-GF.

Remick, Pat. "Myth Is Punctured." UPI, March 8, 1981. www.upi.com.

Russell, Brian. "History: Rocky Mountain Fire Insurance Building and Pantages Theater." https://pantagestheatergreatfalls.weebly.com/history.html.

Sanford, Megan. "A Beacon Upon the Horizon: The Black Eagle Big Stack." The History Museum & Research Center. https://www.greatfallshistorymuseum.org.

Montana Newspapers and Journals

Anaconda Standard
Great Falls Leader Daily
Great Falls Leader Weekly
Great Falls Tribune Daily
Great Falls Tribune Semiweekly
Great Falls Tribune Weekly
Sun River Sun

Books and Other Sources

Carlcaburu, Linda K. ed. *The Big Stack. Great Falls Tribune*, 1982.

Cheney, Roberta. *Names on the Face of Montana: The Story of Montana's Place Names.* University of Montana, 1971.

Frohlicher, S.V. *Stone Age to Space Age in 100 Years.* Cascade County Historical Society, 1981.

Furdell, William J., and Elizabeth Lane Furdell. *Great Falls: A Pictorial History.* Donning Company, n.d.

Gibson, Paris. *The Founding of Great Falls.* Tribune Printers, 1914.

Great Falls City Directories.

Great Falls High School. *The Round-Up 1923.* 1923.

Great Falls Public Schools 100th Anniversary.

Hallsell, Troy. "'It Could Have Been Worse': Great Falls, Malmstrom Air Force Base, and the End of the Cold War." *Montana: The Magazine of Western History* (December 1, 2022).

———. "'It Is Encouraging to See This Much Progress': Malmstrom AFB and Civil Rights Activism in Great Falls, Montana, 1947–1984." *Montana: The Magazine of Western History* (March 1, 2024).

———. "'This Wealth of Woodland in the Desert': Parks and Trees in Great Falls, Montana's Early Development, 1883–1916." *Montana: The Magazine of Western History* (March 1, 2021).

Larson, Regina R., and Viola Williams Stahlecker. *Great Falls Public Schools 100th Anniversary History Highlights.* N.p., n.d.

Montana Historical Society. MC281 Box1, File12. Montana Federation of Colored Women's Clubs, records, 1921–78.

Montgomery, George. *The Years of George Montgomery.* Sagebrush Publishing, 1981.

Moynahan, Jay. *Red Light Revelations: A Glance at Great Falls' Lusty Past, 1889–1918.* Chickadee Publishing, 2007.

Peavy, Linda, and Ursula Smith. *Full-Court Quest: The Girls from Fort Shaw Indian School, Basketball Champions of the World.* University of Oklahoma Press, 2008.

Peterson, Don, and The History Museum. *Great Falls.* Arcadia Publishing, 2010.

Porter, Sister Francis Xavier, and Kristi D. Scott. *Ursuline Sisters of Great Falls.* Arcadia Publishing, 2012.

Robison, Ken. *Cascade County and Great Falls.* Arcadia Publishing, 2009.

Swartout, Robert R. Jr., ed. *Montana: A Cultural Medley.* Farcountry Press, 2015.

Thomson, Janet, ed. *Early Settlers of Great Falls, 1884–1920.* 2 vols. Great Falls Genealogy Society, 2012.

Vrooman, Nicholas C.P. *"The Whole Country Was…'One Robe'": The Little Shell Tribe's America.* Drumlummon Institute, 2012.

Works Progress Administration. *Great Falls Yesterdays.* WPA, 1939.

INDEX

O

P

R

S

T

U

V

W

ABOUT THE AUTHOR

Ken Robison is a native Montanan and a chronicler of neglected Western history. He is a trustee on the board of the Montana Historical Society and has been honored as a Montana Heritage Keeper. He is the historian for the Great Falls/Cascade County Historic Preservation Advisory Commission and the Overholser Historical Research Center in Fort Benton. Ken is a captain after a career in naval intelligence. His most recent books include *Historic Tales of Fort Benton*, *Historic Tales of Whoop-Up Country: On the Trail from Montana's Fort Benton to Canada's Fort Macleod* and *Cold War Montana: From Stolen Secrets to the Ace in the Hole.*

Visit his website, Ken Robison History, at https://www.kenrobisonhistory.com.

Author in Civil War Union infantry officer uniform during a Fourth of July parade through downtown Great Falls. *Author collection.*